THE UCS WORK-IN

THE UCS WORK-IN

by

Willie Thompson

and

Finlay Hart

Foreword by

Jimmy Reid

1972
LAWRENCE & WISHART
LONDON

ISBN 0 85315 265 9

Printed by Farleigh Press Ltd. (T.U.), Watford, Herts.—24580

CONTENTS

FOREWORD

Being close to and so intimately involved in the struggle as I have been is sometimes a disability in taking an objective view of all the events that were part and parcel of this movement. The dust of battle has not yet subsided, and in a certain historical sense I hope it never fully does. However, historians cannot wait while every nuance of the significance of a struggle is clinically evaluated before putting pen to paper.

Be that as it may, there can be little doubt that the struggle of the UCS workers, the unique form of struggle against redundancies and closures that we devised, the almost unprecedented support received from the working class movement and the wide community, is of historic importance.

The two authors of this book, Finlay Hart and Willie Thompson, are to be congratulated on what is the first attempt at a definitive analysis of the struggle. My friend Alastair Buchan produced an excellent book in the midst of the campaign which recorded how events unfolded in the early months of the contest. It was impossible at that time to draw all the appropriate conclusions. In this book at a time when the struggle must be nearing finality, the authors have endeavoured to draw such conclusions. My belief is that their analysis is by and large a correct one. The future may require that judgments made be modified, but I am certain that these will be modifications, not re-evaluations.

If this be so then the authors have performed an outstanding service in producing this book at this time. That there will be other books written on the UCS is certain, but I find it difficult to believe that anything produced in the next year or so can possibly be better in terms of analysis and conclusions than this one.

UCS is part of our contemporary history, its story written by workers and their deeds. It is more than that—it is a portent of things to come. Workers will determine the future and in the process will write the most glorious pages in the history of our country. If there is anything I would wish to add to the account given in this book it is to re-emphasise again the immediacy of the comradeship, humour and wit of the shop stewards and the workers that was such an important ingredient in the struggle and the victory.

JIMMY REID
18 May 1972

1

THE LAMED DUCK

One of the first things you notice about the skyline of Glasgow or Clydebank is the cranes—gaunt yet massive steel monsters that seem to stride across the bleak horizon like an army of giant mechanical soldiers. These bizarre structures stand guard over what have been for more than a hundred years the foundation of Clydeside's economic life—the shipyards with their associated engineering establishments.

Building a ship is something that involves literally thousands of workers and a multitude of skills; welding, plumbing, engineering, draughtsmanship, joinery, painting, electronics etc., etc. A modern ship is one of the most complex pieces of technological equipment in existence. Apart from those workers directly involved in constructing the vessel, hundreds more are engaged outside the yards in producing and transporting components. It is calculated that in the upper reaches of the Clyde today, between ten and twenty thousand workers are dependent for employment in one way or another upon the shipyards. Add to the breadwinners their families, and some appreciation can be gained of shipbuilding's significance here.

To a visitor entering a shipyard for the first time, everything appears to take place on a larger than human scale. The cranes tower above him, the sheds in which the first stages of construction are carried out look like colossal caverns, more appropriate for the workshops of fairytale giants than for mortal men; the noise is overwhelming. Immense plates of raw steel are first blasted with fine steel shot and sprayed with anti-corrosive before being laid out for cutting to specification. Sections are assembled and welded, taken out and lifted by the cranes to their place for fitting into the ship growing on the stocks.

At the beginning of 1971, five shipyards remained of the many that had once existed on the Upper Clyde, four in

Glasgow and the fifth, John Brown's in Clydebank, a separate town of some 50,000 inhabitants, but geographically speaking, largely a continuation of Glasgow on the north bank of the river.

Of the four Glasgow yards, the two furthest upriver, Fairfields and Stephens, lie close to each other on the south bank in the adjoining districts of Govan and Linthouse. Further downriver, but this time on the north bank, are to be found Connell's and Yarrow's in the western part of the city. A mile or so beyond Yarrow's we arrive at Clydebank. As our story begins all these five yards were part of a single consortium, Upper Clyde Shipbuilders Ltd. though one of them, Yarrow's, was, as we shall see, in the process of quitting it.

On the Clydeside, 1970 had not been a year to remember with any joy or affection. Unemployment stood at record levels, and with a Tory Government returned that June, showed little prospect of diminishing.

More than once the threat of closure had hung over UCS and massive redundancies had occurred in the yards. Yet as 1971 opened, the prospects for the yards appeared definitely brighter than they had done for several years. A backlog of unprofitable orders had been worked off, a new order book of sound and profitable contracts had been established, the recurrent financial crises seemed to be things of the past. Labour relations had improved out of all recognition, productivity had achieved an all-time high level, and according to its chairman, 'the company is gaining in strength and morale as each day passes.'

But even as the situation appeared to brighten, sinister political omens could be observed. For several months the Government had been refusing to follow its usual practice of guaranteeing shipowners against possible losses on ships ordered from UCS. It had become stated Government policy to permit the liquidation of "uncompetitive" businesses, regardless of their size or prestige. Rolls Royce and the Mersey Docks and Harbour Board had already gone bust; by February, Westminster was rife with rumours that UCS's turn was coming. To undertake the destruction of an enterprise like UCS would seem, from the point of view of an ordinary human being, to be a piece of lunacy or worse; nevertheless the idea fitted in very well with the strategy of this particular Government and its leaders.

At the head of the administration stood Edward Heath, the first Tory leader to have been elected by his colleagues instead of being selected according to the former practice of backstairs intrigue. What sort of man had the Tory M.P.'s and influential Party chiefs chosen, now become Prime Minister on a minority vote and contrary to all the predictions of political commentators and public opinion polls?

The semi-scurrilous bi-weekly *Private Eye*, having christened Heath "The Grocer", spares no effort to depict him as an egotistical, ignorant and malicious trifler. More sympathetic journalistic sources make him out to be a man of principle, a skilful and determined fighter for what he sees as the good of the nation. It may be so, may be, for we have no way of telling; seldom has a public figure appeared to his audiences so devoid of personality. His speaking style is ponderous and dull, the words trundle from between his teeth, pronounced as if he spoke them with a stone underneath his tongue. The content of his address is invariably soporific, banal, unless the "enemies of the state", Communists, strikers, "violent" pickets are being denounced. Then the voice rises, the delivery becomes more definite though no less monotonous, the cheeks flush and the eyes gleam. But the anger still appears to the observer to be false, a synthetic production turned on for the occasion, or, at the most, as petulance and injured innocence.

In the first Cabinet of this Prime Minister the two men most concerned with industrial affairs were Robert Carr, the man from Securicor, Minister of Employment and Productivity, who played little or no public part in the UCS drama; and the Secretary for Trade and Industry, Mr. John Davies. Heath had imported Davies into his Government specifically to ballast it with business brains and experience. Davies was a former president of the Confederation of British Industries, but whatever his capabilities as a businessman, he proved himself a washout as a politician. For a Government that intended to pursue a policy of extreme attachment to business interests, the logical personality for such a position would have been some wild buccaneer of the boardrooms, a man full of fire and energy, a demonic character over whom the monied classes could have enthused and ecstatically recognised as the embodiment of their dreams and fantasies, one who would have publically delighted in bashing the working class at every opportunity. Davies was precisely the opposite, a man who seemed to have no real idea of what he was doing, to be in a state of complete bewilderment at the antagonism he generated, to be mutely begging for sympathy in the sea of hostility surrounding him. On his visit to Glasgow at the beginning of August, immediately after passing the death sentence on UCS, he tried to shake Jimmy Reid's hand. That was typical of Davies. A man who in his working life had known nothing but the easiest of circumstances simply *could not understand why* he was disliked.

In a number of ways, Heath's Cabinet is strangely reminiscent of the Cabinet of Neville Chamberlain in the 1930's, with whom indeed, the political relic Sir Alec Douglas Home provides a direct link. A band of singularly colourless personalities, pursuing a thoroughly disastrous line of policy with malignant determination, the inferior calibre of its personnel is no accident in either case, but a symptom of the low level to which a bankrupt and decaying social and economic system had reduced its political representatives.

That the system of the "mixed economy" pursued since 1945 was indeed in serious difficulties was a fact universally confessed, though not necessarily in these exact words. It had meant an economy mostly under private ownership run for private profit, but with considerable state backing in loans, subsidies and other forms of assistance, cheap inputs from the nationalised basic industries, free wage bargaining, combined however with a crippling armaments burden and massive financial speculation abroad. By the mid-1960's this was visibly breaking down, with roaring inflation, continual balance of payments crises and industrial stagnation.

Various solutions were advanced from different political quarters. The political Left, through the *Morning Star*, *Tribune* and similar journals, called for an extension of public ownership, a drastic cut in armaments expenditure, and measures to at least clip the wings of the financial wizards. From another standpoint, Harold Wilson put his faith in the "technological revolution" and regarded fundamental social reconstruction as unnecessary. The conservative trend represented by Enoch Powell had an entirely atavistic approach of return to a 19th-century style economy, and though Heath's government and the mainstream of conservative thought was rather more sophisticated it showed many of the same elements.

Nobody can say that the Government did not give fair warning of its intentions, summed up in the very revealing phrase of John Davies himself regarding "lame ducks". Direct government subsidy to private industry would be phased out so far as possible, allowing "merciless competition" to weed out the "backward and inefficient". This "lame duck" approach was, of course, being aimed at some massive combines—Rolls Royce, for example, not to mention UCS. But it was basically a policy bound to favour the larger monopolistic industrial and financial units at the expense of the weaker sectors who also traditionally support the Tories; and therein lay a danger. Smaller businessmen would tend to discover that without adequate financial resources or access to masses of capital they too would be stigmatised by the Government as "lame ducks". But their support might still be held, in spite of this, by Government action to introduce "freedom" into the labour market, a project dear to all Tory hearts, whether monopolistic or not. Enoch Powell had openly declared that trade unions and industrial action were absolutely useless for raising wages or anything else. The legislation which the Government brought in did not actually forbid them, but its Industrial Relations Act represents a far-reaching attempt to cripple independent militant trade unionism and reduce it to an instrument of government policy. The Immigration Act, which was the next proposed piece of major legislation, would act in the same direction, discouraging immigrants from industrial action and setting black and white workers against one another.

The Government approach to UCS was therefore not an isolated specimen of meannesss or spite, nor did it follow from misunderstanding or ignorance in distant Westminster of the true situation on Clydeside. It was simply all of a piece with the general outlook and philosophy of these politicians, the political guardians of big business.

We now introduce the reader to the Hon. Nicholas Ridley, under-secretary to the Minister of Industry Sir John Eden, and a central figure in the events leading up to the liquidation of UCS. Mr. Ridley derives from an impeccable Tory background, being the younger brother of the fourth Viscount Ridley and a member of a family long connected with the ownership of coal and steel in north-east England. The nationalisation of these two industries did no great damage to the family wealth, but probably helped to inspire in Nicholas his profound hatred for public ownership displayed in a paper submitted by him early in 1968 to a conservative study group, in which he went even further than official Tory policy in advocating the hiving off of profitable parts of nationalised industry.

Late in 1969 Mr. Ridley, then Opposition spokesman for Technology, had visited Clydeside, and after a very short discussion—said to have lasted only one hour—with his Tory shipbuilding friends, notably Sir Eric Yarrow, had composed the now notorious "Ridley Memorandum" recommending a Government "butcher" to carve up UCS, hive off Yarrows and sell cheaply whatever remained saleable to private enterprise. The process which the Government put into motion in early 1971 followed almost exactly the lines of this document, though Davies later claimed never to have seen it until it came publicly to light.

First of all, Yarrows were extricated from the consortium, a movement which had been in process since mid-1970 but was only now completed. The naval shipyard, having received a covered berth and other advantages from the merger, was now provided with another £4½ million to see it on its way. On the same day that Davies announced Yarrows' separation, February 11, he also made it plain that no new public funds would be made available to UCS, a point which he repeated with emphasis a month later, presumably in case any creditors had missed it the first time.

It is interesting to note at this point UCS were *not* asking for any fresh funds.

The effect of the statement was to start a landslide of creditors' claims and a refusal of further credit. Cunard now chimed in with a writ for £2 million for alleged delays on the Queen Elizabeth 2. The claim most probably had no legal validity whatever, but it helped to worsen the public image of UCS in the eyes of its creditors and suppliers.

Very quickly the money ran out, and in June the management were obliged to make their way to England to submit a request for a further £6 million government loan. On June 14 Davies in the House of Commons turned them down in an atmosphere, according to Paul Foot in *Private Eye* No. 249, of "cheers and laughter from his backbenchers", and the Board immediately applied for a provisional liquidator.

As the Clydeside workers, with massive public support, were preparing to fight back, the Government, congratulating itself on its generosity in undertaking to keep the yards going until August 6, commissioned a report on their future by a specially appointed committee—the "Three (later four) Wise Men."

These individuals, all well renowned for their sympathy with and understanding of the working-class point of view, were Alexander McDonald, Chairman of the Distillers Company; Sir Alexander Glen the shipping magnate; David MacDonald, director of the merchant bankers Hill Samuel (all good Scottish surnames!), and jolly Robens, chief liquidator of the English, Welsh and Scottish coal industries, ex-chairman of the

National Coal Board and once, allegedly, a socialist.

In their fine impartial fashion these gentlemen laid all the blame for the crisis upon the work force—or upon the management only insofar as it had not been rough enough with its employees, asserting that it had not "exercised efficient control of costs, particularly wages, which in their impact seriously threatened other industry on the Clyde". This last was presumably a reference to the fact that rates of pay were somewhat higher at UCS than in the Scott Lithgow group on the Lower Clyde. Understandably, the Lower Clyde shipyard workers resented the situation and, using UCS as a comparison, had been pressing for wage increases. This competition by UCS against Scott Lithgow in the labour market, as well as its competition in the market for orders, was an additional reason for the intransigent hostility which the Lithgow group had always shown (and still shows) to the Upper Clyde.

The "Four Wise Men" went on to recommend that "any continuation of Upper Clyde Shipbuilders in its present form would be wholly unjustified, and would cause serious and more widespread damage".

Therefore UCS should go into liquidation with a loss of seven jobs in ten, reducing employment from 8,500 to 2,500, closing the Clydebank and Scotstoun yards, with a successor company at Govan/Linthouse. Even this last was to be provisional on the acceptance by the workforce of double dayshift working and "competitive" wage rates—i.e. wage reductions.

The honesty of the Tory Government and its confidence in its four investigators can be gauged from the fact that it kept all the evidence on which these conclusions were based a dead secret and has continued to do so ever since.

On July 29, as Davies rose in the House of Commons to announce his acceptance of this scandalous document, the labour movement in the West of Scotland had already been mobilised to the accompaniment of a gigantic demonstration and stoppage of work. The following day the work-in began.

2

THE BACKGROUND—BRITISH SHIPBUILDING IN CRISIS

The distress of UCS was only the most spectacular example of the general plight of British shipbuilding by the end of the 1960's. It is impossible to understand how the industry had got itself into this mess unless we appreciate some aspects of its development over the previous century, in particular the shocking story of greed, shortsightedness and incompetence on the part of the owners. Naturally, the report of the "Four Wise Men" made no reference to this, preferring, in line with Government thinking, to treat UCS as an isolated lame duck.

In the beginning, British shipbuilding set out with tremendous advantages. When iron, and later steel ships began to replace wooden hulls from the middle of the 19th century onwards, Britain was the only country industrially developed enough to supply them in the necessary numbers, and with the gigantic expansion of trade which occurred in those years, these numbers multiplied prodigiously. During the 1890's no less than 80 per cent of the world's steam ship tonnage, amounting to just under one million tons per year, was built in British yards. These yards were located naturally beside suitable waters for launching, in the vicinity of iron and steel producing centres; two such areas became especially predominant—north-east England and the rivers Tyne, Wear and Tees, and Clydebank. Together they accounted for by far the greater part of the tonnage launched.

The progress of the industry was closely associated with the developments connected with imperialism, colonial expansion, the search for new markets and military rivalry. The kind of ships, and their sizes, both for war and for trade, affected the growth and development of shipbuilding. The skill of the pioneers of marine engineering helped these developments. By a combination of factors the Clyde became the premier shipbuilding river in the world early in the last century. It retained that proud position until affected by the general crisis of capitalism that followed the 1914-18 war. Of the four yards that now form the UCS consortium, each have a long record and made big contributions to the naval and mercantile history of the British fleets.

The Clydebank Division

The world famous Clydebank shipyard was established on a green field site in 1870 by the Thomson Brothers and was sold to John Brown & Co. the Sheffield steelmakers, 20 years later. Up until the end of the second world war it held the record of having built the world's biggest liner, and the largest aircraft carrier.

Scotstoun Division

The yard of Charles Connell & Co was established in 1861. It was known in its early days as the "convict yard" because of the reforming zeal of the owner, who engaged ex-convicts, and not because of the prison-like conditions under which shipyard workers toiled in these early days. Connell's was one of a number of yards that did not have its own engine work. Its record was established as builders of fast sailing ships. Since the beginning of the century it has had a very fine record and is a modernised yard.

The Govan Division

The Govan Division of UCS is composed of two shipyards, Fairfield's and Stephen's. Fairfield's Shipbuilding and Engineering Co in 1885 took over the shipyard of John Elder and his successor Wm. Pearce, who were associated with the early developments of the steam ships. Both have left their mark in Govan. Some of the most modern ships are Fairfield built and the yard, with the men who work in it, are steeped in the traditions of shipbuilding.

The neighbouring yard, Stephen & Co. Ltd., had a remarkable history of shipbuilding and engineering. The Stephen family were associated with shipbuilding for more than 200 years before being taken over by the UCS. A member of the Stephen family began shipbuilding in Burhead on the Moray Firth. Later generations of the family built ships in Aberdeen, Arbroath, Dundee. In 1851 Alexander Stephen leased the Kelvinhaugh shipyard but 18 years later bought the Linthouse estate and established the yard that became world famous as Stephen's of Linthouse.

The shipbuilding yards described, with the addition of one other, Yarrow & Co. Ltd., are all that is left of a once thriving expanding industry on the upper reaches of the Clyde, whose products have penetrated every sea and inland lake throughout the world.

Nevertheless, built, as they were, into what were already major industrial centres, the yards everywhere in Britain, tended to be small, cramped and poorly planned. In nearly every instance they were run by "family firms" in which, though shares might be publicly bought and sold, control was concentrated in the hands of, and exercised by, a tight family oligarchy. Although, by the miserable standards of the time, shipbuilding was a relatively highly-paid industry, working conditions were extremely bad, work being carried on out of doors with very few amenities and worst of all, being subjected to violent cyclical unemployment, as demand for new tonnage has always tended to fluctuate immoderately, more so than for most commodities. Trade union organisation was likewise deficient; about forty different unions eventually came to represent the various trades involved, and large pockets of non-unionised labour remained up to World War II.

Labour and Management Relations

It has been recognised throughout industry that the shipbuilding employers were and are among the most hard-faced men in their relations with their workers. Every advance that has been made in wages and working conditions has had to be fought for. There has always been a considerable amount of casual labour in shipbuilding. At the various stages of a ship's construction, if there was not enough work on other ships, to which men could be transferred, the men were paid off. The construction of the hull of a ship mainly absorbed the labour of the "black squad"—that is the name for shipyard boiler-makers. Launching dates for most of these men coincided with pay-offs. Then it was the turn of the finishing trades. They took over the fitting out of the ship. When the ship was handed over they went on the unemployment list until another hull had been prepared for launching. With the exception of the two world wars, that has been the lot of the shipyard worker.

It was the casual nature of the work that aggravated the conflict among shipyard workers on lines of demarcation. If the shipyard plater or shipwright, the plumber or engineer, could establish their exclusive right to perform certain operations in the building of the ships, their chances of avoiding the recurring payoffs were better. The older men in the industry remember the insistence of the employers, long ago, and they would now like it forgotten, that crafts should be sub-divided. Every trade had its experts at particular operations. That resulted in, e.g. the boilermakers' craft being sub-divided into separate trades, each man serving an apprenticeship with no right to do the operations for which he was not time-served.

This is the perspective against which we must evaluate the vapourings of Lord Robens & Co on the "failure of managements to exercise efficient control of costs, particularly wages."

By 1914 over a million and a half tons (not including warships), were being launched from British yards. Over a fifth of this was exported, in spite of the fact that foreign yards had also been making substantial headway at the beginning of the 20th century. The achievement was due, above all, to the skill and craftsmanship of the underpaid and maligned shipbuilding workers, for technically, the firms, grown complacent, had failed to keep up to date, being content to milk their depreciating fixed capital for all it was worth in favourable market conditions where they could scarcely fail to make profits.

Their inadequacies were brutally exposed in the course of

World War One, when their backwardness prevented them from being capable of replacing the tonnage sunk, in spite of labour dilution, new government established shipyards and standardisation of ships.

These are the points which have to be kept in mind when we read in the report of the "Four Wise Men" that the UCS was composed of "five companies whose shipbuilding competiveness was exceedingly doubtful", and that "facilities remain . . . ill-equipped and cramped". In the succeeding years these shortcomings were to be compounded even further by the owners.

In the years following World War One the consequences of their sins fell upon the shipbuilders, or rather upon their unfortunate employees, who were made to bear the brunt of the abysmal crises into which the industry now plunged.

The problems of technical inadequacy were speedily aggravated by intense competition from foreign builders, particularly German and Japanese. The expansion of diesel propulsion, to which the British marine-engine builders were unaccustomed, occurred in a situation of general decline in world trade—hence in demand for merchant shipping. Following a last frantic boom in 1920, during which two million tons were launched,—the highest ever figure from British shipyards—the general crisis of the capitalist economy during the interwar years set in, characterised above all by massive unemployment and a phenomenal level of unused capacity in every industry. In 1921 orders for 300 ships were cancelled; during the 1920's unemployment in shipbuilding never fell much below 20 per cent—real wages were lower than they had been in 1914.

In the 1930's came the worst phase of the 20-year crisis, starting with the collapse of the U.S. stockmarket in 1929. The level of world trade plummeted to new depths, freight rates sank. By 1933 unemployment in British shipbuilding had reached 63 per cent—not counting the thousands who had left the industry, and in that same year only 131,000 tons were launched. The "Queen Mary" rusted for months on the stocks, being completed eventually only because of government intervention.

Faced with this situation, only one answer occurred to the owners of the yards and their backers in the banks. This was to "rationalise" the industry and attempt to restore profitability by restricting competition, to be accomplished by the physical destruction of every "uneconomical" yard, leaving the available orders to be divided among the remainder.

In 1930 the National Shipbuilders Security Ltd was formed at the instigation of, and under the Chairmanship of, one James Lithgow of the Port Glasgow firm, to buy up bankrupt yards and "sterilise" them for forty years by reselling them under a restrictive covenant prohibiting their use as shipyards. By this means, capacity for over 1¼ million tons annually was dismantled at a cost of £1¾ million. Compensation was received by the owners of the plant affected but nothing was given to the men thrown out of work. The yards closed were not necessarily by any means even the most antiquated, but were those in financial difficulties. The most notorious case of all—Palmers at Jarrow, was a well-equipped enterprise. Seldom has the greed and lack of foresight of the capitalist class been revealed with less inhibition. Even such an orthodox commentator as Professor G. C. Allen describes it as an "egregious folly", and doubts whether it brought any overall benefit to British shipbuilding in the 1930's even from an employer's viewpoint, though it certainly strengthened the position of the dominant firms, who, all through this period of intense distress and decay, seldom failed to pay a dividend.

The Contribution of the Clyde Yards

During the economic depression between the two great wars, Clyde shipyards, famed for their ships, their technique, and the high quality of their products, disappeared. They were the victims of unplanned capitalism, of greed and refusal to invest part of their profits in the new techniques that modern science has developed in ship construction. Great names associated with shipbuilding on the Clyde have disappeared. National Shipbuilders' Securities in 1938 scrapped McMillans of Dumbarton, Napier and Millars of Old Kilpatrick, Beardmores of Dalmuir, and what was known as the Belgian yard, Whiteinch. It was deliberate economic sabotage. The policy indeed nearly had disastrous consequences in World War Two, yet the governmental system of control then in force over shipbuilding was exercised through the same James Lithgow and other shipping magnates of equal ill-fame. Profits of 5 to 10 per cent were realised by the main firms in the course of the wartime emergency. Shipbuilding was not, unfortunately, made a candidate for nationalisation by the Labour Government in 1945.

Paradoxically, the war was to give to the shipbuilders another chance—their last.

The plant of the major competitors, Germany and Japan, had been destroyed in the course of hostilities. By 1949 the percentage of world tonnage built in British yards had recovered to 45 per cent and employment had regained 1914 levels. This coincided with the growth of an apparently insatiable demand for shipping as the war-ravaged economies recovered and world trade boomed. The major component of this growth lay in oil-tankers—the demand for which grew by 10 per cent every year up to 1957.

The shipbuilding magnates, however, continued obstinately in their former disastrous practice and lived only for the day. They proved utterly incapable of taking advantage of the uniquely favourable market situation and while the yards worked at full pressure with full order-books, their backward and antiquated technology, inadequately renewed, failed completely to capture an additional share of the expanding market, or even to maintain what it had. The output of British yards never rose above 1½ million tons in any year, hardly in excess of the wartime figures. By 1954 the British share of world building was down to 27 per cent—two years later to 21 per cent—and in that same year the country lost its position as the world's premier shipbuilder, being overtaken by Japan. No real effort was made to meet the challenge; the restrictions of the Shipbuilders Securities, partially relaxed during the war, were actually reimposed in the years following it.

This wretched performance produced its inevitable consequences. When the boom ended in 1958, British shipbuilding was launched once again into profound crisis, and by this time a further sinister element had made its appearance—the growing tendency of British shipowners to place their orders abroad. By contrast, most of the industry's foreign rivals followed a policy of compulsory home construction for their national fleets and furthermore laid out lavish subsidies to their shipbuilders, a practice eschewed by British governments at this time.

In the early 1960's a spate of further closures took place, many of them on the upper reaches of the Clyde. All of the yards affected there had made a considerable contribution to the world's stock of ships, past and present. Dennys of Dumbarton, the inventors of ship's stabilisers, Barclay Curle of Whiteinch, the two yards in Renfrew that specialised in building dredgers that are now performing in most of the world's harbours and rivers all disappeared—Harland and Wolff closed their Govan Shipyard where many of the Palestine Oriental fleet were built. Harlands had taken over the Pointhouse yard at Partick and closed it, too. With the closing of Hendersons at the mouth of the River Kelvin where it flows into the Clyde, there were destroyed connections that were amongst the earliest pioneers of shipbuilding on the Clyde. This tragedy of the Clyde is an indictment of the failure by an owning class who have always been among the most violent opponents of nationalisation in any form. They would rather destroy than allow these yards to become the property of the nation.

In 1963, launchings were once again below 1 million tons and this British share of the world total had declined to 11 per cent.

The revival of the market in the mid-sixties brought little relief, for by then attention was being focused on the giant tankers and bulk carriers, ships which were, ton for ton, cheaper to build and operate than their smaller predecessors, but which the British yards were quite unfitted to construct.

Confronted with this situation, the Labour Government in 1965, advancing as always in the white heat of the technological revolution, appointed the Geddes Committee to investigate the industry. R. M. Geddes, O.B.E., who had proved his ability for this task in his successful career as a soft drinks manufacturer, duly presented his report in February, 1966.

The main point of its proposals was a solution to the problems of the industry conceived entirely in terms of capitalist rationalisation, amalgamation of the units, concentration of production, high productivity and reduction of the work force.

As the Communist Party, alone of all political parties, was quick to point out at the time, the only solution adequate to the depth of the crisis was reorganisation of the industry under nationalisation in the interests of its workers and the people generally. But the Labour Government accepted the principles of the Geddes Report, which were, by and large, implemented in the following four years, and under the authority of the newly established Shipbuilding Industry Board, extensive rationalisation took place, the Clyde yards in particular being reorganised into two consortia, the Upper and Lower Clyde groupings.

In spite of this, in spite of the large sums of government money poured like water into the owner's hands, in spite of the tens of thousands of workers discharged, 1970 found the British industry with only 5 per cent of the world tonnage in a market which, despite fluctuations, was growing steadily and apparently without limit; and scarcely more competitive than the firms had been five years earlier. In essence, the developments in British shipbuilding of the late sixties mirrored those of the thirties.

These are the considerations which the "Four Wise Men" left entirely out of account. At every stage in its development the industry has been crippled by the greed and incompetence of its owners. While things went well, they failed to carry out the necessary re-investment and renewal to keep their fixed assets up to date; in time of recession they embarked on programmes of running-down and the destruction of productive resources, both human and material. Their thirst for profit was boundless, and matched only by their failure in imagination and lack of foresight.

What has it all meant for the shipyard workers in terms of unemployment, anxiety and frustrated hope scarcely bears thinking of. At every crisis the pitiless barons have expected the workers to bale them out, by working harder for less reward or by removing their unwanted presence from the scene.

One of the principal demands of the "Four Wise Men" upon those who were to be permitted to retain their jobs was that they should accept double dayshift working, including a shift from 2 p.m. to 10 p.m. Quite rightly this was something the men had always resisted bitterly; such hours, it can be readily imagined, are utterly destructive of civilised living, and leave scarcely any free time unless the person involved is willing to sit up between twelve and six in the morning. It is to be wondered whether any of the four gentlemen in question would be willing to work such hours, but they were ready to demand it of others—and wage cuts into the bargain—otherwise "a total cessation of shipbuilding on the Upper Clyde". Indeed, it may well be that in the present crisis British capitalism is ready to let the entire industry, not only the Upper Clyde, go down the drain.

Certainly such a solution has been canvassed in the pages of their financial press. It is no longer "profitable" and scarcely worth extracting from its troubles. The respective fates of the *shipping* and *shipbuilding* industries make an instructive contrast.

The former is immensely profitable, based on the to-date, never-ending expansion of world trade and low wages for its employees. But the shipowners have no worry about productive potential—they can go to the fresher and better-designed yards of foreign builders while British shipbuilding is left to rot and die. After all, that is the most profitable solution!

3

THE CRISIS IN CONTEXT

The extent and the violence of what the Government had intended to do can only be fully grasped when it is appreciated what part shipbuilding and its associated industries play, not only in Britain as a whole, or in relation to the working class of the U.K., but in a specifically Scottish context. This was much more than an issue affecting only the Clyde valley, or just another move in the Tory industrial strategy. It was a brutal challenge to the entire Scottish nation and a crippling blow aimed at the head of the entire Scottish working class.

For the size of its population, 5.2 million, Scotland occupies a relatively large area, but the gross figures are misleading, for no less than four-fifths are packed into the central industrial belt, and even within this highly populated area there is an especial concentration in the western region, which contains over 47 per cent of the country's total, Glasgow itself having nearly a fifth (just under one million) and Clydebank comprising a town of 50,000 inhabitants, while the Clydeside conurbation as a whole falls just short of 2 million.

In addition to this very high degree of geographical concentration, Scottish industry is concentrated in yet another manner, owing to the fact that it includes, compared to the national average, an unusually high proportion of the staple industries, of which shipbuilding is only one. The others include heavy engineering, textiles, mining, metallurgy, and the predominance of these trades in the Scottish economy records the fact of Scotland's critical role in an earlier stage of British industrial development. In the 19th-century not only was the Clyde the world's premier shipbuilding river; Glasgow was, in addition, Britain's greatest manufacturer of railway locomotives—no trace of which achievement remains today.

The slump which affected shipbuilding in the interwar years was not, of course, an isolated phenomenon, but one aspect of the general crisis the economy was passing through in this period. Among the most outstanding features of the crisis was the disproportionate way in which the basic industries suffered. At an earlier stage of industrial history they had dominated the world market; owners had taken full advantage of that piece of good fortune to milk them dry, using the profits for more immediately attractive purposes such as foreign investments. In consequence, renewal of the industrial base was hopelessly neglected, and the basic industries emerged from World War One quite unfit to compete with foreign industrial rivals for the world markets on which they had formerly depended and which were, withal, shrinking at this period. As a result their degree of unused capacity and their unemployment levels during the Depression were higher than those of any other sector of the economy.

As would be expected in such a situation, the areas of Britain where these trades predominated in the industrial structure suffered with particular severity, Scotland included, where unemployment levels at all times stood well above the national average.

In 1944 the Scottish Committee of the Communist Party published a memorandum on shipbuilding which envisaged the retention and expansion of the industry and the harnessing of it to the needs of the people instead of to private profit. This had always been the basic Communist approach during the difficult inter-war years, and to that end the Party had set the pace in calling for the nationalisation of the industry and of shipping itself. The memorandum started from the position that trade could be expanded enormously in the post-war years. This would create increasing demand for new ships. And to meet this, it was suggested that the work in the main shipbuilding centres should be co-ordinated with a national plan for the whole industry and that there should be standardisation within the particular yards. Had these policies been pursued, the subsequent crises in the shipbuilding industry could have been avoided. But this was not to be.

Certainly, following World War Two the basic industries

enjoyed a period of renewed demand for about fifteen years, but as we have seen was the case with shipbuilding, the 1950's found them once more in crisis (though in a lower key than had been the case in the 1930's). The problems inherited from that earlier period had not been overcome; their profitability was lower than that of more newly developed industry; there was property speculation and financial manipulation, and government policy was simply to allow them to contract until they found their "economic level". In the case of nationalised industry this could be brought about by direct government interference, as with coal and railways; in those still under private ownership, like shipbuilding or textiles, it simply meant a lack of government support and neglect of any measures of planning.

The Scottish economy, being strongly orientated towards just these industries, was among the principal victims, and the results were very serious. The staples, finding themselves in a difficult market situation, began to shed labour and Scottish unemployment figures rose, until during the 1960's it was hovering around 5 per cent on average, well above the British figure, and some pockets far worse still.

Wages in stagnant industrial sectors failed to keep pace with those elsewhere; Scotland became in due course a low-wage area. The chronic sickness in the basic industries reflected itself throughout the whole Scottish economy, retarding growth and rendering development much more sluggish than it need have been.

Deprived by such circumstances of attractive opportunities, many of the most active population were driven beyond Scotland's borders, seeking their chances in booming south-east England or abroad. In spite of a birth-rate which is significantly higher than the British average, the Scottish population has scarcely increased at all during the past decade; chronic depopulation is one of the country's most severe difficulties.

It is now accepted wisdom among economic commentators that the roots of the Scottish economic crisis lie in the central role played by the "old" industries, allegedly "trades of a traditional nature that have long since lost their dynamic." They claim that it is the industrial *structure* which is wrong, and that a heavy reliance on such industries must without fail produce the drastic economic sickness with which Scotland is plagued, for, so it is said, these industries are bound to decay and will, unless replaced, drag the Scottish economy and Scottish living standards down with them.

The regional policies pursued by governments since the 1960's have reflected this governing assumption; the idea has been that the basic industries should be phased out and replaced with others having greater growth potential—electronics, office machinery, vehicles, for example. Thus, only very timid steps have been taken to arrest their decline. Of these, the most significant has probably been the obligation laid upon the South of Scotland Electricity Generating Board to use coal-fired rather than oil-fired generation, so retaining a market for the Scottish coal industry. This was accomplished, however, only under vigorous pressure from the miners, and it did not save 75 per cent of the Scottish pits existing in 1950 from being closed down by the National Coal Board, and the labour force being cut from 101,000 to 55,000 between 1950 and 1967. In privately-owned shipbuilding an exactly similar trend is evident, with numbers employed falling from 73,000 in 1950 to 50,000 in 1967, while tonnage launched from Scottish yards declined in the 1960's by approximately 40 per cent.

The steps taken by various governments to replace the failing industries by other forms of development were, as is admitted on all sides, scarcely adequate. Basically, what "regional policy" amounted to during the 1960's was a programme of subsidy by the government of capital costs—and eventually labour costs as well—to any industrialist who could be persuaded to set up in certain specified "development areas". True, that was better than nothing and did make some contribution towards alleviating the problem, but apart from being insufficient to mop up the unemployment, it involved no real planning or efforts to achieve a balanced economic structure. If the businessmen didn't want to come in spite of the inducements, there was nothing to make them do so.

The fallacy behind this sort of thinking lay and still lies in the unquestioned belief that the basic industries are superannuated and must die, and the only alternative is to promote the development of light industry. It is true that they could not "stand on their own two feet" in market terms, but the "market" is not a natural or accidental phenomenon, it is the product of policies and decisions on the part of monopolist businessmen and government ministers. For example, the fuel market is determined by the deliberate government decision, made under pressure of the oil lobbies, to promote (except in a few cases) oil at the expense of coal; the shipbuilding market is shaped by the fact that foreign governments heavily subsidise and protect their shipbuilders; the British government did not do either of these until it was too late.

In short, there is no *inherent* reason why the basic industries should be liquidated. A sensibly planned programme of economic development, making the best use of our natural and human resources, would find a place for expansion in *both* the old and new sectors, and the gigantic human and material capital represented by these industries would not be light-mindedly jettisoned in order to gratify the thirst for profits of a few millionaires and monopolists. Such was, indeed, the programme put forward by the Communist Party in 1960, *Shipbuilding, Looking Forward.*

The Tory governments of the fifties and early sixties, and the Labour governments which followed them were, setting aside their different motives, sufficiently concerned about the menace of unemployment to try to keep the process in check, and while incapable of tackling the problem at its roots, at least tried to prevent it from getting out of hand by trying, as indicated, to induce new industrial development and to keep the disintegration of the basic industries progressing at a sufficiently slow rate to prevent the chronic ailment of unemployment from assuming acute dimensions.

In 1970 Edward Heath in a notorious remark promised the public a "new style of government", and Tory intentions soon became clear enough. John Davies philosophised on lame ducks and at the same time regional policy was modified, with the promise that major incentives would be phased out by the mid-seventies. In other words, the staple industries which, due to previous neglect and policy, were severely distressed in any case, would be left to rot and ameliorative measures would be cut back.

The vast regional problems which Scotland had been confronting for many years had been tackled with inadequate machinery incapable of ensuring a genuine solution. A "Plan" drawn up by the government in 1966 for overall economic advance was abandoned almost as soon as printed. Under the Tories that serious situation was threatened with a catastrophic deterioration, and shipbuilding lay at the heart of the matter.

For Scotland, as for the other regions in economic peril, the implication of this Government's attitudes were terrifying. If all industries which could not show unaided a profitable balance sheet were to be allowed to go the wall, a very considerable section indeed of the Scottish economy was doomed—coal, shipbuilding, mining, agriculture, to mention only the more obvious. In addition, the economic devastation caused by such collapse, the colossal unemployment, the total loss of confidence in the area which must result, would unquestionably sink the new industries and other profitable sectors into the bargain. Enoch Powell, the apostle of this sort of policy, expressed the opinion that Scottish workers had no right to expect work to be provided for them in Scotland: they should migrate to wherever employment was available—a pronouncement in conflict, to say the least, with his usual sentiments on migration.

What threatened Scotland was, in sober reality, nothing less than national destruction, but there was no need to wait until the axe had been laid to all the national industries to appreciate what was likely to happen. Shipbuilding alone provided a sufficient foretaste of the future if the Tories got their way. Its elimination would suffice to tear the heart out of the west-central region, in many ways the economic pivot of Scotland.

As well as being economically central, however, it is also afflicted by some of the most severe social problems in Britain. The connection is not accidental—the social problems are a direct result of its dependence on heavy industry, giving rise to the economically depressed status of the area, which has never, owing to this fact, been able to overcome entirely the grim heritage of the industrial revolution and the 19th century.

The housing problem in Glasgow is notorious, both in terms of the number of inadequate homes and the extent of deficiencies—overcrowding, damp, lack of facilities. Every now and then the sudden collapse of a tenement creates a temporary press sensation. As fast as slums are cleared new ones emerge to replace them, and the rehousing programme has been, over the years, planned badly. The rehoused population is concentrated in a belt of housing estates—schemes as they are known in Scotland—surrounding the centre of the city. In these are to be found not a cinema, not a dance hall, not even a pub, no public amenity of any kind, a situation which is a direct inspiration to vandalism and the formation of juvenile gangs. Moreover the tenants of local authority housing in Glasgow are further harassed by the Tory government policy of steadily pushing rents upwards.

In the lives of half-a-dozen generations the effect of Glasgow's housing situation on personal self-respect, on the destruction of family life, in promoting anti-social behaviour and alcoholism, in the creation of bitterness, despair and loss of hope, is one of the blackest pages in the record of British capitalism.

In the field of education, especially in the working-class areas, Glasgow is probably one of the least favoured areas in the entire country, depending on numerous antiquated schools and suffering a crippling teacher shortage.

Over it all looms the shadow of unemployment, bad enough in itself, but also to be considered as an aggravating factor, intensifying all the social problems encountered in the Clyde valley. The conditions we have outlined are themselves an affront to human dignity: to be confronted with unemployment as well puts those faced with such a prospect in a situation which words cannot express. We have to try to imagine the 10 per cent male unemployment already existing in this area reinforced by the numbers who would have been made redundant through the UCS closure. The mind boggles.

As for Clydebank, it stood to become the Jarrow of the seventies, "the town that was murdered". It is scarcely less dependent for its livelihood on John Browns than Jarrow was on Palmers. The town itself is very similar to Glasgow in architectural appearance; in fact it is a continuation of the city. A hill slopes northward from the river, and at its foot, fronting the water, lies the yard. Parallel to the river we find the rather narrow main street and only major shopping centre, with county buildings and a municipal library that contains fascinating historical material on the town's past. Across the road lies Singer's sewing machine factory and the large Co-op bakery together with some smaller enterprises. At right angles, the other major streets run straight up the hill, where, apart from cinema and Technical College, most of the remainder of the town is residential as we continue uphill, until on the outskirts and adjoining north-west Glasgow we encounter the housing scheme of Faifley with its two Communist councillors.

The people of Clydeside have unique culture and tradition, formed out of their response to the harsh and bleak industrial environment in which their lives have taken shape and of which the heavy industries and especially shipbuilding are the ultimate economic foundation. They have absorbed it and shaped it to their own purposes, as the Eskimos have made the bitter arctic deserts the principle of their existence and culture, and they weren't going to let anybody snatch it away from them. Alongside the sharp, self-deprecating irony expressed in so much Glasgow humour and repartee, the traditions include equally a refusal to be mucked about by the purblind powers-that-be, and a strong political element. In all likelihood, the nature of that political heritage was one reason why robber Heath and his not-so-merry men decided to pick on this area and this industry.

4

HOW UCS FELL

We turn now to the establishment and financial collapse of the UCS consortium, and here the report of the "Four Wise Men", hitherto unsatisfactory, becomes outrageous. So far as the long-term background is concerned the Report, as we saw, ignored it entirely, but in relation to the years since 1968 it is worse, infinitely worse. Its one thousand or so words contain an extraordinary series of distortions, misrepresentations, and outright untruths. As Anthony Hepper, the UCS Chairman was to declare later: 'I think it is one of the worst reports I have ever heard. . . . The first part is to my mind superficial and biased. It consists of a series of assertions unsupported by factual evidence and interlaced by statements which are wildly untrue.'

The UCS consortium had its origin in two events: the Geddes Committee report of 1966, and the struggle to save the Govan yard of Fairfields from closure in 1965, an action which had important precedents for the struggle today.

In October 1965 the affairs of this shipyard were put in the hands of an official receiver. Learning from the lessons of the Simon Lobnitz closure in Renfrewshire two years previously, a campaign was mounted on the Clyde to save Fairfield's—a campaign that exceeded all precedents in the mobilisation of shipyard workers in the West of Scotland.

The yard had launched three ships totalling 55,000 tons and had £131 million worth of orders for new ships. Moreover it had been completely modernised and, from the public's point of view, looked like one of the most prosperous yards on the river. To allow the banks to close a going concern like Fairfield's was more than the workers in it were prepared to stand.

Their call for support was answered by every shipyard and engineering establishment on Clydeside. In all of them, meetings were held to voice total support for Fairfield's, and joint consultations took place between their representatives and those of the threatened yard to discuss common action. The Scottish Trades Union Congress called a special meeting of union officials attended by Roy Mason, the Minister responsible. The M.P.'s in the area were alarmed at what damage could and would be caused to the contracted shipbuilding industry and took part in the campaign of publicity and representation to the Government.

With massive strike action not excluded as an ultimate resort, the Government, by November 1965, was compelled to do something. With £131 million of orders tied up and the mounting temper of the men in the yards, the Chancellor of the Exchequer authorised a Bank of England advance of £1 million to keep the yard in operation until the early spring.

In the meantime the Government was negotiating with an industrialist, Mr. Iain Stewart, Chairman of Hall Thermotank and a director of seventeen other companies, for the setting up of a consortium to run the yard. This consortium was to be composed of the Government plus private enterprise with some trade union participation. Naturally such activity raised the question of the Government itself taking over the yard as a going concern. Private industry had obviously failed, but Mr. Roy Mason refused to consider nationalisation, declaring that "the country cannot afford to pension off sick industries, our resources are too scarce for such a policy", thus anticipating in his own way John Davies' "lame ducks" attitude.

Nevertheless, Fairfields was saved. It escaped the fate of its neighbour Harland and Wolff's Govan yard, now nothing but a wilderness with no vestige of its previous achievements to be seen. This happier outcome, it must be remembered, was accomplished only because the shop stewards, supported by the rest of the workers on Clydeside, took a stand against the decision to close the yard, and the lesson was not forgotten.

Thus it was that Fairfield's became one of the constituents of the merger promoted by the Shipbuilding Industry Board, which brought Upper Clyde Shipbuilders into existence in February 1968.

However, Yarrows continued to maintain a semi-separate existence, the consortium possessed only 51 per cent of Yarrows shares, and this firm, unlike any of the other units, maintained its own Board of Directors within the merger.

For the other three companies, though, the unification took place just in time to save them from very considerable embarrassment—that of probable bankruptcy. John Browns, Alexander Stephens (which had not had an order for nearly two years) were all in an extremely rickety state—under-capitalised and apallingly managed, whether from the point of view of their work force or even that of efficient capitalism. These firms were now able to discard their individual liabilities under the umbrella of the new undertaking backed by public money, while at the same time keeping a tight grip on their more desirable assets. John Brown's profitable engineering works, for example, situated right next door to the shipyard, did not become part of UCS: it was hived off from the merger.

In the words of Iain Stewart, Chairman of Fairfields and original Deputy Chairman of UCS: 'I think without the merger John Browns would have gone bankrupt, and Connells and Stephens were probably heading for bankruptcy too. That was why they were in such a hurry to get into the merger.' (*The Times*, June 24, 1971).

The ownership structure was as follows: John Browns 30 per cent, Connells 5 per cent, Stephens 10 per cent, Yarrows 20 per cent and Fairfields 35 per cent. This gave the Government a 17 per cent stake in UCS by virtue of its 50 per cent ownership of Fairfields; later this was to be increased to 48½ per cent. The unions likewise, by their participation in Fairfield, were also part-owners, but in contrast to the "Fairfield experiment" no union representation was permitted on the new Board. In addition, the consortium was brought to birth with a sinister inheritance, accumulated losses of something like £12 million from the mismanagement of previous years.

The "Four Wise Men" dwell with great emphasis on the acknowledged shortcomings—the losses, the debts, the fact that, as a single enterprise, the five yards made a rather unwieldy conglomerate structure. They go on to accuse the company of a "mistaken marketing policy which led to losses on new contracts."

At best, this statement shows astonishing ignorance and an unbelievably frivolous approach to what the four were supposed to be examining; at worst it is a deliberate lie. All commentators agree that the losses of £8 million or so on *new* contracts were incurred *before* mid-1969 when Ken Douglas took over as Managing Director. The backlog of unprofitable orders was eventually worked out, so that by 1971 it was one of the few shipyards in the world to have an order book composed of ships taken on at current prices. This order book, at the time of liquidation, was worth £90 million, with many more orders in the pipeline. The £90 million of orders comprised 34 ships with a total deadweight tonnage of around 172,000 tons, sufficient to keep the yards working for several years. Not only that, but a complete realignment of building policy was undertaken under which the construction of unprofitable specialised ships such as the "Queen Elizabeth 2" was dropped, and emphasis placed instead on building standardised bulk carriers and general cargo vessels. In the latter class, a new design was evolved and announced late in 1969. This was the multi-purpose "Clyde" ship of 14,750 tons deadweight, giving more cubic capacity, high speed, increased container capacity, greater deadweight, better cargo handling and a faster turn-around. This was further developed by 1971 to give the faster "Super Clyde" vessel of nearly 20,000 tons dwt. A much larger design, the "Panamax", of 67,000-75,000 tons for passage through the Panama Canal, was brought out at the same time. The press predicted almost unanimously a bright future for these designs, especially the "Clyde" in which an eager interest was shown by various shipping lines. Nine were building or on order at the moment of liquidation.

In the light of these facts to say, as the Report does, that ". . . . the total injection of public funds has disappeared. No improvement in facilities, no worthwhile investment has been made. . . ." is totally absurd, and again, some of the most pertinent facts are ignored. On its formation UCS received a loan of £5½ million interest free for three years from the Shipbuilding Industry Board, but of this, £3½ million went to pay off losses on existing contracts; i.e. public money was used to bail out the former owners. Only £2 million remained available for investment and of this more than half went to build a covered yard for Yarrows, the unit which was least attached to the consortium and half-owned by one of its bitterest opponents—Sir Eric Yarrow.

We now come to one of the knottiest problems of them all—labour relations. Traditionally the shipyard owners have made every effort to shuffle off the blame for their own deficiencies on to their workforce, and their efforts to get this story publicly accepted has been perhaps the most successful of their enterprises. Who can think of shipbuilding without immediately envisaging endless tea-breaks, preposterous demarcation disputes, absurd wage claims and all the rest of it? The only shortcoming in this picture however, is its complete divorce from reality. In 1925 a joint committee of the shipyard unions and the employers noted that the best British tender for a particular contract would have been uneconomic *even if the men on the hull had worked for nothing*, and in 1938 the *Glasgow Herald Trade Review* gave this as the general position regarding British and foreign prices. Things change very little. K. S. Reader in his book *The Modern British Economy* (Longmans), points out that wage differences between Britain and Japan today make very little difference to the price of a ship and observes that "failure to anticipate change in the 1950's was the prime cause of the difficulties of the British shipbuilders in the 1960's."

Before the UCS was formed, wages in shipbuilding were negotiated at national level between the Shipbuilding Employers' Federation and the Confederation of Shipbuilding and Engineering Unions. These negotiations determined the national uniform plain time rates, hours, overtime, allowances, travelling time, etc. At yard level, the respective unions negotiated along with the shop stewards on the piecework and bonus rates. Discontent had been expressed over the years at the wide variations in wage rates between yards and between shipbuilding areas. One thing that stands out in particular in the relations between the UCS management and its workers was the amicable solution of wage differentials that had always seemed impossible in previous negotiations with the individual yard owners.

There were fifteen separate unions responsible for wage negotations on behalf of their members, consisting of skilled, semi-skilled and unskilled workmen. After the National Agreement had been substituted with a UCS agreement all differences between management and men were settled without having recourse, as in the past, to district and national conferences. The only union that still insisted on taking any dispute through the old negotiating procedures if there was failure to agree with the UCS management was the Boilermakers.

All concerned agreed that, as proved by experience, the new procedures were a big improvement over previous practices. There is additional evidence here that those who decided to cut down had not examined the potential future for the consortium arising out of the new labour practices, or if they had, didn't give a damn. The statement of the advisory committee that "management had not exercised efficient control of costs, particularly of wages" can be seen for the nonsense that it is. They admit an improvement in productivity (though concealing its dramatic extent—87 per cent in steel throughput) but go on to say that "this improvement does not offset the inherent weaknesses in the present structure and facilities of UCS." What evidence do they offer for this diagnosis? None whatever.

UCS' big affliction, which the Government consistently exploited in order to bring it down, was its shortage of ready working capital. It was recognised from the start that several years must elapse before the concern could hope to pay its way. During the intervening period it would be necessary above all to ensure that sufficient credit was available to maintain supplies to the yard. Every business survives on credit, as usually costs must be met before (often long before) payment is received in return, but in shipbuilding this applies with particular force. It can take years to complete a ship and all the while the yard must continue to carry the costs of materials, labour, overheads, etc.

From start to finish the UCS was crippled by never having sufficient of this vital working capital, while being obliged to pay out £2 million annually in loan interest, and no organisational ingenuity on the part of the management nor sacrifice by the labour force could compensate for it. Every so often the company was obliged to come pleading to the Government for assistance; assistance was given up to 1971, but in miserly dribbles and never up to the amount that was required, which had the effect of forcing the management always to come back again within a comparatively short time, and frequent requests created the impression that public funds were being poured into a bottomless sink.

An adequate provision at the beginning would have eliminated the need for continuous applications, but this was deliberately withheld, first of all by Anthony Wedgwood Benn when Minister of Technology. He also refused John Browns in 1969 when they offered their remaining shares in UCS to the Government. Acceptance would have meant virtual nationalisation, but here, as in so many instances, the Labour Government dodged its responsibilities.

The following year fresh government assistance became necessary, but was secured only after the unions, and especially the Boilermakers, had been blackmailed by threat of closure into accepting 3,500 redundancies, while shipbuilding was discontinued at Stephens, which now became a steel fabrication plant. Although by 1971 the management thought that, consequent on these sacrifices, they had rounded the corner and achieved commercial viability, they had not quite made it, and the need for continuing government support was, as we have seen, the principal lever used by the Tories to overthrow the firm.

Perhaps our accusation that the Government deliberately drove UCS into a corner may be thought a little extreme, but all the evidence certainly points in that direction, including Davies' own statement that the Government could not go on indefinitely handing out money to bankrupt enterprises. In this case though, the Government itself was almost wholly responsible for the bankruptcy, and its refusal of guarantees (not even money) to the consortium between October 1970 and February 1971 prevented the acceptance of orders which would otherwise have been forthcoming, then their restoration in an atmosphere of panic and alarm, provoked the final collapse.

Yet the management in June asked Davies for only £6 million. Having refused, the Government then agreed to pay £3 million to keep the yards going until its committee had reported—already 50 per cent of the required amount. Add to that redundancy payments, social security benefits, unemployment benefit, etc. etc. The figure far exceeds already the modest sum required to keep the yards going. £10 million is a conservative estimate of the *direct* costs of liquidating UCS, but the indirect costs extend far beyond this.

In addition to those made redundant from the yards we must not forget the wave of bankruptcies and closures which would have immediately followed among the suppliers. In the final analysis, it is likely that something like 30,000 people would lose jobs directly or indirectly, and so far as social cost can be transferred into monetary terms it has been calculated that this was likely to be something approaching £100 million—an expensive price to pay for a lame duck to shoot! (see *UCS The Social Audit*, published by the Institute for Workers Control).

These are the results which would have followed from the recommendations of the "Four Wise Men." Of these recommendations they had the gall to declare: ". . . . in view of the Government's share of responsibility we have also given weight to social considerations which we believe the Government must in this case observe."

5
THE WORK-IN BEGINS

A hot summer morning in July. Outside the massive gate of John Browns shipyard, positioned at the end of Clydebank's main shopping street, a knot of newspaper reporters wait expectantly—it is known that the proposition of a workers' takeover has been put forward in answer to the Government's announced intention to accept the report of the "Four Wise Men".

Then, without warning, the gates are pushed open, the security men are told politely that their functions are now superseded by the shop stewards, and the pressmen are invited inside to witness the mass meeting of over 3,000 workers being held just outside the manager's office.

Jimmy Reid, spokesman for the stewards, is addressing the meeting, announcing the first campaign of its kind in the history of British trade unionism.

What manner of person is Jimmy Reid? Burly and dark in appearance, he is, like most of the people he represents, industrially and in local government, a native of Clydebank, where he passed his childhood during the depression years. These, he recalls, with poverty and unemployment the stuff of daily existence, made a profound impression on him, vividly lighting up the injustice of workless men and deprived families with idle machinery and unused industrial equipment all around.

Ironically perhaps, his first employment on leaving school was in Glasgow stock exchange, but the prospect of a lifetime spent in the direct service of capital being too cruel to contemplate, he returned as an engineering apprentice to John Browns shipyard. Having joined the Young Communist League and led a famous apprentices' strike he left Scotland soon after to become National Secretary of the Young Communist League, a post which he filled with distinction until

1964, but maintained his Scottish connection as Parliamentary candidate for the Communist Party in the East Dumbartonshire constituency of which Clydebank forms a part.

Some months following his return to Scotland, Jimmy Reid was elected Scottish Secretary of the Communist Party, meantime returning to live in Clydebank's Faifley housing scheme, where in 1969 he was elected as the burgh's fourth Communist councillor. He has for many years been a member of the Party's National Executive Committee.

In late 1969 personal circumstances led him to resign from the Scottish Secretaryship, and he returned to his trade in John Browns, where he was rapidly entrusted with the responsibilities of shop steward.

Now he winds up his speech with defiance to the Government in the name of the shipyard men and of all Clydeside:

'We are taking over the yard because we refuse to accept that faceless men can make these decisions. We are not strikers but responsible people. We will conduct ourselves with dignity and discipline.

'There will be no hooliganism, there will be no vandalism, there will be no drinking. . . .' and ends, to cheers:

'We don't only build ships on the Clyde, we build men . . . and Davies has taken on the wrong people'.

The people whom Davies had taken on have a remarkable tradition of industrial militancy and determined resistance to government injustice. The engineers and shipbuilders of Clydeside were well to the fore in the massive wave of strikes that shook British capitalism to its roots in the years before World War One. Here was to be found the main stronghold of the Socialist Labour Party, one of a number of revolutionary political parties active in Britain at that time, and numbering among its members the Irish socialist and patriot James Connolly. This party suffered from a number of deficiencies which inhibited its development, such as uncompromising hostility to the official trade union movement, but produced a remarkable body of devoted socialist propagandists and working class organisers.

During the years 1914-1918 it was on the Clyde that the working class resisted most fiercely the efforts of employers to use wartime conditions as the excuse to impose "patriotism" on them in the form of wage cuts and worsened conditions, while the bosses filled their pockets. Here the national shop stewards' movement had its birth, led by engineers such as Willie Gallacher, and it was in Glasgow that the legendary socialist agitator and educationist John Maclean developed—at the cost of recurrent prison sentences for "sedition"—a formidable opposition to the useless bloodletting and imperialist objectives of that war.

In the immediate postwar years, as during the course of the war, Glasgow was the scene of violent and bloody clashes between the forces of "law and order" breaking strikes and committing social injustice, and the labour movement resisting them. At one point the city was occupied by tanks and soldiers, at another, strikers fought a pitched battle with police in the main city square. Even in the thirties, the grimmest years of the depression, Clydeside maintained its record, and it was, once again, out of its shipyards and engineering shops that another industrial action of major significance began in 1934, the apprentices' strike, which in spite of massive unemployment and the intransigent hostility of employers and public authorities succeeded in winning a new deal for young British workers.

In spite of all the many far-reaching social and political changes which have taken place since 1945, Clydeside remains as fundamentally working-class in its outlook as ever. If voting in Britain had always followed the same pattern as in Scotland the Tories would never have been in power again after World War Two, and nowhere in Scotland is Labour more strongly entrenched than in the west. Glasgow in the General Election of 1970 returned only two Tory M.P.s; since the war the Labour Party has dominated its Corporation. "Tory" was such a dirty word that in local elections the conservatives had taken to calling themselves "Progressives".*

* Though some of them in the past few years have now begun to fight under an open Tory banner.

Though special circumstances have occasionally produced a "Progressive" majority it has always proved ephemeral. Clydebank is an even more solid Labour stronghold; no Tory whatever sits on its Council, but in 1970 there were four (now three) Communist councillors, including Jimmy Reid. The workers in the heavy industry of the region were the living foundation of this anti-Tory fortress.

The Government therefore had plenty of motive for beginning its exercise in lame-duck hunting in this area. In Westminster Tory eyes, the Clydeside must have appeared not only outlying and far away, not only inefficient and uncommercial, but stiff-necked and insubordinate into the bargain, and therefore doubly ripe for learning the hard lessons of social security and dole queues.

Without any doubt the Government strategists had aimed their assault primarily at the working class, hoping that the damage inflicted in Scotland might have repercussions throughout the labour movement. They were right too, though hardly in the way they had anticipated, for the implications of what they had done, affecting circles of the Scottish population far beyond the labour movement, raised a remarkable degree of solidarity throughout Scotland. Immediately the decision to liquidate had been taken, the men and their leaders, building on the experience gained in the fight to save Fairfields, moved to establish the broadest and most far-reaching resistance to the Government's intentions, drawing in local authorities, the church, M.P.s, the Scottish Trades Union Congress and various other civic institutions and prominent individuals.

The Glasgow Trade Union Centre is the headquarters of Glasgow Trades Council and an immensely popular social club. It is situated on one of the most attractive spots in Glasgow's centre, where it shares premises in an elegant building fronting the south bank of the river. Legend has it that this building, with its plain and well-balanced 18th-century appearance, was the original design for Glasgow's Town House, but was rejected in favour of the rococo monstrosity that now dominates George Square.

It was inside a large meeting-room in the Trade Union Centre that stewards from the four yards convened on Sunday June 13, and first adopted the idea of direct action in the form of a work-in to prevent the yards from being closed. The idea, we are told, had emerged over the weekend in discussions between some of the stewards searching for an initiative that would be a sufficiently effective and dramatic riposte to the announcement of liquidation. It was put to the meeting by Sammy Barr, the convenor of stewards at Connells. At first the idea was received sceptically, even with a hint of ridicule by some, but as the implications of the proposal started to sink in the mood changed. It was pointed out and accepted that straightforward strike action would be inappropriate in the circumstances; in a situation of liquidation it would only enable the liquidator to put up the padlocks all the quicker. Perhaps a sit-in strike then? But that would be almost impossible to maintain for the exceptionally long drawn-out battle that was in prospect, especially in view of the geographical spread and scatter of the work force over the four yards. A work-in would, on the contrary, hit the enemy from an unexpected direction, would lay the basis for the widest possible public support and circumvent the problems involved in the other two forms of action, while by assuming control over the gates it would publicise the struggle and the men's determination in the most dramatic fashion possible.

However, it was not for putting into immediate execution. It was necessary first to see how the government would move, and whether it would listen to reason from Clydeside's representatives. The stewards made immediate arrangements to send a delegation to London to confront the Prime Minister. The following day, Monday 14, after a mass meeting of men in the yards had endorsed the stand taken by the stewards, the Clydebank Town Council resolved to charter a special train to London, the Provost, Mr. Robert Fleming, remarking —how truly—that the British Government was now trying to do to Clydebank what the Nazi bombers had failed to do during World War Two. Glasgow Corporation followed quickly with the decision to dispatch representatives for the same purpose, as did the Scottish Trades Union Congress.

In the course of the following week Heath was obliged, though reluctantly, to receive deputations from the UCS workers, the civic authorities, and the S.T.U.C. Nevertheless his ears were shut tight against the force of their arguments and Jimmy Reid was obliged to report, with some asperity, that 'I got the impression that we were talking to men who did not know what it means to stand in a dole queue, or what it can mean to working class families, and worse, who didn't seem to care'. He added, 'we were prepared to applaud any concession the Government might make, but in the absence of any such decision we reiterated that we are going to fight—not only the shipyard workers but all the workers are going to fight . . .'. Willie McInnes, convenor from Linthouse, put it even more shortly: 'They will need to get the soldiers from the Bogside to get us out of the Clydeside'.

The pledge made by the stewards on behalf of the workers and people of Clydeside was implemented promptly; on Monday June 21 plans were laid for a token industrial stoppage and mass demonstration through the streets of Glasgow. These plans were drawn up at a meeting of representatives from all sorts of mass organisations throughout the West of Scotland, including 800 shop stewards, trade union officials and clergymen of several denominations.

Although later overshadowed by the even more phenomenal turnout of August, the demonstration on the afternoon of Wednesday June 24 was a most impressive affair, to say the least. Over 100,000 stopped work, and half that number marched in Glasgow, led by the stewards, several M.P.s and the entire Town Council of Clydebank. The march included representatives from every factory in the West of Scotland as well as delegations from over the border; for example, Carlisle Trades Council sent a delegation. According to some it was the biggest demonstration ever outside London.

The rally which followed at Glasgow Green heard Jim Airlie, Chairman of the Shop Stewards' Co-ordinating Committee, report that the workers in the shipbuilding industry would not stand for any closures nor any contraction in the existing labour force, and listened while Anthony Wedgwood Benn regretted not having nationalised UCS while the Labour Government was in power and read out the draft of a nationalisation Bill which he had just introduced in the House of Commons, sponsored jointly with Willie Ross, the ex-Scottish Secretary, William Hannan, chairman of the Scottish Labour Group of M.P.s, William Small and Hugh McCartney.

Unfortunately this expression of popular indignation and of united resolve in the labour movement was treated with contempt by the Government, which proceeded, as already noted, to declare on July 29, through the mouth of John Davies, its irreversible intention of executing the consortium.

A deputation of shop stewards from the Co-ordinating Committee met Mr. Davies on the previous day in his room at the House before he attended the Cabinet meeting at which the final decision was taken. Davies made it clear to the delegation that there would be redundancies, and that these would be considerable. He was warned by the shop stewards that any contraction of the shipbuilding industry would precipitate a struggle not seen in the political life of this century.

The men had returned from holiday to work in the Clydebank Division on the Monday preceding Davies' statement. The Govan and Scotstoun divisions were still on holiday. Prior to their going it had been agreed that the shop stewards and their Co-ordinating Committee would be alerted in the event of any change. The meeting that had decided to send the deputation to see Davies also agreed that shop stewards should be in the Govan and Scotstoun yards when the future of their establishments was being decided.

The day of the announcement the atmosphere in Clydebank was one of stunned shock. "Like a town in mourning" the *Glasgow Herald's* reporter described it. 'The worst we have ever feared has now happened", said Mr. Fleming the Provost bitterly, detailing the hardships which must fall forthwith upon the town as a result, and ending, '. . . Many local shopkeepers will be forced to close almost immediately because they cannot meet their rates. This will be a progressive thing, a form of local economic cancer. . . .'

Within a very short space of time however, dismay had given way to determination—on the part of the workers as expressed by Gerry Ross, a boilermakers' shop steward in the yard, who declared, 'If there is to be any contraction it will be over our dead bodies. We are better to die here in the yard than to be starved into submission at the labour exchange'.—and on the part of Clydebank's citizens summed up in the declaration made by William Neville, a Labour councillor: 'I think if the workers occupy the yards it will be a very effective demonstration, and there is no doubt that they are very determined men. They are going to fight and I think every last man, woman and child in the town will support them'.

So on Friday July 30 the shop stewards took over control of three yards. There was no violence or resistance, and the police had promised in advance not to interfere. Men and materials entering or leaving the yards came under the jurisdiction of the stewards who manned the gates. Every four hours a group of stewards took over responsibilities that had previously been the job of the security men.

This is the point at which we left our newspapermen, who were able to listen to Jimmy Reid's speech only because the stewards had countermanded the orders of Mr. R. Courteney Smith, now fully established as Liquidator, who had tried to exclude press and television from the mass meeting.

In the course of the next fortnight the strength of the movement backing the UCS men expanded rapidly. A repeat, on a bitter scale, of the strike and demonstration that had taken place in June was planned for August 18. These plans were laid before a meeting in Glasgow on August 10 attended by over 1,200 shop stewards from all over Scotland and the north of England, which unanimously endorsed the plan and appealed to all workers to give financial support to the work-in. Six days later the Scottish Trades Union Congress convened the first special congress in its history.

It was to be expected that the entire trade union body and its co-ordinating organ would swing solidly behind the UCS. Cutting out the country's industrial heart, as the Government plainly intended to do, meant, as a corollary, the disembowelling of its labour movement. The effect of mass unemployment on trade unionism is always very negative. Funds obviously suffer, for out-of-work men cannot give their union the same financial support as they can when employed. Industrial claims and actions are much more difficult to conduct when many hands are stretched out for few jobs; worst of all disillusion and despair strike at the membership, undermining confidence in their organisation. The immediate effect of the closure of UCS would be, in Tory eyes, to create a huge and cowed force of jobless shipworkers, a gigantic industrial reserve army exerting a downward pressure on the wages of those still employed at Yarrows and the Lower Clyde; while, as the resulting closures multiplied their way through the shipbuilding suppliers and industry at large, the same effects would generalise themselves in the Scottish labour movement as a whole. When a government deliberately intends to use *crisis* as a weapon to combat the economic difficulties of Great Britain, sacrificing in the process millions of workmen and even thousands of minor employers, its hand is only stayed when vigorous counter-measures are mobilised against it.

This emergency congress of the S.T.U.C. represented a significant step in the mobilisation of support, as indicated by the standing ovation with which Jimmy Reid was received when speaking on behalf of the stewards, for the meeting resolved unanimously on financial and other support, particularly to throw its efforts into the strike and demonstration planned for August 18.

That Wednesday turned out brilliantly hot. 'No doubt at all whose side God is on', as one demonstrator was heard to remark. It is estimated that a quarter of all Scottish workers, about 200,000 in all, downed tools that day. The starting point for the demonstration was George Square, which is spacious but by early afternoon had become far too limited to hold the crush of marchers and spectators who had begun to spill over into adjoining streets.

Three o'clock has been set as the starting time, by which point numbers have grown to 80,000 marchers or more. It is the greatest demonstration since the days of the Chartists, some commentators are to claim, and this may well be true, but the labour movement has come a long way since the great and tragic days of 1848. No longer men with "fustian jackets and unshorn chins" (the unshorn chins where they exist are now a badge of fashion not poverty) but men and women whose own struggles, following on those of their fathers and grandfathers, have secured for themselves and their families the beginnings of a tolerable existence. They have laid down their tools on this August day because they are well aware that their modest comforts have been put at risk by a relentless government, and to show their determination to maintain them. Some of the placards, of which a veritable forest is sprouting, are explicit about this point, "No return to the Thirties" they declare, but many more are humorously defiant, "A Harvey Smith to Heath!", and the slogans extracted from his maritime adventures are apparently limitless; "Launch UCS—Sink Heath!"

The paper industry will certainly flourish if the number of leaflets, pamphlets, newspapers and broadsheets changing hands is anything to go by, and the footage of film being shot by amateurs and professionals alike will unquestionably provide rich pickings for future social historians and commemorative television documentaries. On the monetary support pouring in, it is only necessary to quote the words of one steward on the collections: 'This is fantastic. We won't be able to count it all until after the demonstration'.

To a succession of tumultuous cheers the march to Glasgow Green sets off. Marching in the lead with arms linked are Vic Feather, General Secretary of the T.U.C., Hugh Scanlon of the Engineers, James Jack, General Secretary of the S.T.U.C., Jimmy Reid and Jim Airlie, Dan McGarvey, President of the Boilermakers and Chairman of the Confederation of Shipbuilding and Engineering Unions, together with representatives of political parties, Wedgwood Benn, for the Labour Party, Alex Murray, of the Communist Party, and William Wolfe from the Scottish Nationalists. Delegations have attended from every part of Britain, and almost all of them are accompanied by pipe and drum bands, which together with the singing that breaks out spontaneously all along the line greatly intensify the dramatic quality of the scene.

Marchers are still leaving George Square at the time when the head of the procession is forming up in Glasgow Green. The united front being presented to the Government is symbolised by the very wide range of speakers on the platform, the industrial leaders from both inside and outside Scotland, Wedgwood Benn and Willie Ross representing the Labour Party, William Wolfe of the Scottish Nationalists, and Alex Murray for the Communist Party.

James Jack and Hugh Scanlon speak of history, past and future. Scanlon reminds his hearers that Clydeside workers had taken action more than fifty-nine years before to secure recognition for shop stewards; now the Clydeside was out to compel recognition of another principle, the right to work. James Jack asserts that the action at UCS will live for all time in the history of the trade union movement, a milestone on the road to achieving socialism in Britain. Vic Feather emphasises that they are not supplicants on bended knees but trade union stalwarts determined to frustrate the Government's plans for turning the Clyde into an economic graveyard. Speaking on behalf of the Communist Party, Alex Murray draws the following lessons from what had happened:

'The struggle of the UCS workers has many lessons for the working class, including that the fight against unemployment cannot be conducted in the abstract or by words alone, however reasoned. It is the *action* of the UCS workers that has been the catalyst, that has galvanised millions of people into united action in their support. Their action, their struggle, has become the focal point of the struggle of millions of workers throughout Britain'.

The loudest cheers of the day are reserved for Jimmy Reid, whose presence is formidable and whose words are heard with hushed attention.

'The workers in Britain are getting off their knees, getting on their feet and asserting their dignity, asserting their abilities, asserting in a determined and disciplined way that they will have a say in the decision making of this country. . . .

'No-one has the right to destroy the aspirations of the young men or the security of the old men, no-one has the right to demand that people leave their countries if they want work. We started off fighting for our jobs and in a matter of days we knew we were fighting for Scotland and for the British working class movement. . . .

'The real power of this country has been forged today in Clydeside, and will be forged now in the pits, the factories, the shipyards and the offices. Once that force is given proper leadership, is disciplined and determined, there is no force in Britain, or indeed in this world, that can stand against it'.

There is one person who ought to be on the platform but who is not—Sir Donald Liddle, Glasgow's Tory Lord Provost, elected to his office when Labour briefly lost control of the Corporation at the height of public dissatisfaction with the Wilson government. Certainly he has protested at the proposed closure, and urged the Government to think again. No doubt he is sincere, and besides the policy being followed in London will have devastating effects on the many small businessmen and "sweetie-shop Tories" upon whom the Right depend for their support in Glasgow's municipal elections. But he will not back the stoppage and demonstration, for, 'This loss of production in industry is not clever at a time when we are trying to fight for jobs and keep our heads up . . . the effect on production must be very considerable indeed'. His words have no effect on the demonstration, of course, and all he succeeds in doing is to diminish his own credit and publicly to demonstrate the impotence of any effort to dissociate the fight for UCS from the labour movement and its traditional weapons.

The demonstration of August 18 provided an inestimable lift to the morale of the labour movement throughout the country and enormously strengthened the confidence within it that the Heath policy could be frustrated. Nevertheless, the front line in the struggle during the weeks and months that were to come remained in the four yards and with the workers inside them. Let us now enter them and see at close range how it was conducted.

6

MAINTAINING THE WORK-IN

It is an ordinary working day at John Brown's, though "ordinary" is not now perhaps the most appropriate term, for the work-in is now well established, and the final decision on all major issues is firmly in the hands of the workforce.

From the outside, nothing much appears to have changed; traffic is normal in the street, the gates stand open and unattended but for a solitary shipbuilder stationed there, more for the purpose of assisting enquirers than for guardianship against non-existent enemies. Occasionally a policeman will stop by to determine whether everything is in order. It invariably is.

The appearance of placidity and near-complete normality is in no way an indication that commitment is in any way less than it was, rather it signifies the complete opposite; such unity of purpose has been achieved inside and outside the yards that the occasion for turmoil is completely absent.

Laying this granite foundation for the struggle was in many ways the most remarkable attainment of all, and paradoxically some of the credit for it must go to Heath, Davies and Ridley, for it was the recognition of what their proposals meant that melted down certain barriers standing in the way of unified action.

Two conditions in the shipbuilding industry were especially detrimental to the maintenance of solidarity; the heavy cyclical unemployment referred to in Chapter 2, and the growth of very highly elaborated craft division. These combined to create the sometimes very bitter demarcation disputes of the late fifties and early sixties, and the attitudes they gave rise to can be illustrated by the remark attributed to an old welder at the time when rivetting was disappearing as a trade and the rivetters were being retrained as welders: 'Aye, you can give them a welder's torch, and a welder's goggles, and a welder's cap, but they'll never be anything else but damned rivetters.' The most specific of these problems was the widespread feeling among other trades that the boilermakers occupied an over-priviledged position.

The responsibility for these divisions lay upon the irresponsible exploitation and neglect to which the industry had been subject during its history, and the hostilities fomented in the labour force by the old employers in order to strengthen their own position. It was in the course of fighting against the logical outcome of these practices, bankruptcy and closure, that the inner divisions were entirely surmounted.

Circumstances in themselves would not have achieved that, however, had the circumstances not included also the purposeful and clear-sighted leadership which proceeded from the shop stewards and the nerve-centre which they created, the Coordinating Committee that replaced the old Liaison Committee at the commencement of the contest.

Round about forty members, more or less, sat on the Coordinating Committee. It had started off with the four convenors from each yard, the four boilermakers' convenors, four finishing trades convenors and four general workers' convenors along with the chairman and secretary of the previous Liaison Committee. New tasks and responsibilities made necessary the election of additional shop stewards, and in addition six representatives from the staff and middle management were brought on, while an invitation was extended to the full-time trade union officials from the West of Scotland district of the Confederation of Shipbuilding and Engineering Unions to attend the meetings.

Nine in the morning in the classroom of the Clydebank Division was the appointed time and place of the Committee's daily meetings, which lasted on average two hours. The absence of any steward required an explanation from his convenor, but in fact there was little falling-off in attendance during the course of the work-in.

It is easy to outline the formal routine of the Committee, though more difficult to convey what it meant for the stewards who participated or the strength of the confidence with which the men regarded it.

The standard day of the committee began with the minutes of the previous day's business and matters arising, followed by correspondence, reports of meetings with Government ministers, trade union bodies and so on, as well as any questions concerning relations with the Liquidator. Regular reports of the activities of the five sub-committees came up for approval.

The Committee's decisions were transmitted through the yards by a chain of communication that began with meetings between the yard convenors and departmental shop stewards, who then explained them at weekly meetings in their particular department, which also fulfilled the function of informing the stewards, and through them, the Co-ordinating Committee, of any problems arising in the course of the work-in. Anything that could not be resolved at shop-floor level could then be taken up to the departmental management, or if necessary the yard management, through the yard convenor. Questions of principle involving top management or the Liquidator remained with the Co-ordinating Committee.

The central strand in the work-in strategy was the refusal of the men paid off to accept redundancy notices, who instead continued to appear for work as usual. Obviously the Liquidator did not pay them, and the workers themselves became responsible for the continued employment and payment of those he had attempted to discharge. In the allocation of tasks to them, responsibility fell, once more, upon the shop stewards in the various departments; in some cases the foremen cooperated, though in others they did not. In one major respect however, the situation of the men working-in was different from that of their mates being paid by the Liquidator, the apparatus of the work-in was not designed to cope with matters of compensation arising from industrial injury, so the redundant workers being paid by the Co-ordinating Committee were not put on to shipyard jobs involving a serious degree of risk.

When the Liquidator took over the affairs of UCS, the yards continued to process the ships which were under construction at that time. As it was intended to rundown the Clydebank and Scotstoun divisions, no new ships were being laid down to keep up the continuity of work in these yards. As the work advanced, men and staff being laid off and removed from the Liquidator's pay roll stayed at their jobs and reported for work as usual. In co-operation with the stewards and staff, as indicated, they doubled up with their mates still in the Liquidator's employment. The sharing of work in this way presented a particular problem—if the output was doubled then the Liquidator only paid for half of that being done, which meant that the general public, the subscribers to the UCS appeal fund, would be subsidising him and thereby making his job easier. It was decided therefore that when a work-in man and an employee of the Liquidator shared a job, the total output would not exceed the amount expected from the employee. It was, in addition, an inflexible principle of the Committee that no overtime should be worked except for emergency maintenance.

Payment to the redundant workers was based on average earnings prior to attempted dismissal, and these workers received their average pre-redundancy *after tax* earnings, with cards stamped. The gigantic financial operation which this represented, both in fund-raising and administration, was, along with all the other expenses of the work-in, in the hands of the Finance Committee, based at the Clydebank yard and made up of Dan O'Donnell, Willie Robertson, and the treasurer, a welders' shop steward in the Clydebank division, a sharp-featured little man, limitlessly energetic. The best-kept secret of the struggle was in the Finance Committee's hands, the actual value of the fighting fund at any particular time. To know it would have given the Government a tremendous advantage in the war of attrition and enabled it to make a shrewd estimate of its adversary's strength. So it was never revealed—not even to the leaders on the Co-ordinating Committee.

Between £8,500 and £9,000 was paid out weekly, and for keeping the cash flowing the Committee was completely dependent on the solidarity of the labour movement, both British and international, and on the sympathetic public. Its excellent organisation and publicity kept it closely in touch, and from the beginning of the struggle the incoming funds never failed.

Those paid by the Liquidator had details of their time taken from their cards by his staff, but the work-in men had theirs taken by clerks who were paid off and also began to work-in. A dual organisation was in being, which could never have functioned had it not been for the determination of the workers on one hand and the co-operation of the staff on the other.

The first financial resource was in fact the 50p per week which all UCS workers, whether paid by the Liquidator or the stewards, levied themselves. It can be said to the Liquidator's credit in this instance that he made no objection to the use of his computer by the Committee for this purpose, nor did he try to interfere with the use of premises by the Committee at Clydebank yard.

Thus the bread-and-butter affairs of the work-in in the yards themselves were organised by the Co-ordinating Committee with an unexampled smoothness and lack of friction. Naturally, difficulties and problems did arise from time to time; the UCS workers are not supermen; but it is indicative of the conditions and feeling prevailing in the yards that they were invariably settled after amicable discussion with goodwill on all sides, and no issue of this sort was ever permitted to grow to the stage where it made a report in the press.

In the sphere of the vital decisions of principle and strategy arising at every stage of the action, the Co-ordinating Committee must go beyond the relatively simple aspects of its day-to-day management and operate its leadership through the elemental democracy of the mass meeting. Surely no word has suffered more abuse in our century than the term "democracy". It has been used as a cover time and again for intolerably anti-democratic practices and institutions. Edward Heath claims in justification for his behaviour that he represents the democratically elected government; his understrapper, Anthony Barber, as he conspires to keep the railwaymen miserably underpaid yells rhetorically, 'Who will govern the country? The democratic government or the sinister monopolistic unions?'

Recent governments in this country have done much to devalue the democratic processes which they boast of as their national pride. The gap between government and the community has grown very wide. The citizen-in-the-street finds that his vote and free speech is no protection against being subjected to the sort of catastrophe represented by the UCS liquidation.

Not least of the achievements of the fight-back has been the new breath it has put into the concept of democracy, the practical schooling it has given in the combination of mass participatory democracy with effective and responsive central leadership. Jimmy Reid has told us that the mass meeting is without question the main channel of communication between the stewards, represented by the Co-ordinating Committee, and the men in the yards.

A mass meeting of the UCS workforce at one of the yards is an unforgettable spectacle. A specially organised fleet of buses bears the contingents, amounting to several thousands of individuals, of the yards who are travelling. Platforms and loudspeaker equipment have been erected, from which, as the arrivals troop in, pour jokes and folk-songs, laid on by performers among the men themselves.

In a way, these workers are fortunate to be shipbuilders; this sort of democracy would be materially impossible in most establishments, for few of them have premises of sufficient size to accommodate such a meeting. In a shipyard, though, there is plenty of room. Seven times between August and the following February, the workers massed below the platform, forming up into disciplined and orderly congress, well aware on each occasion they so met that their own futures, the future of Scottish shipbuilding and of Clydeside hung on their continued unity and the good sense of their decisions.

A crowd, at its lowest level is nothing more than a large collection of individuals. As he takes his place in the assembly each participant is first of all himself, locked away inside his own skull from his neighbours and fellows. Behind his eyes, as they now focus upon the stewards mounting the platform, there passes who knows what hopes, fears, desires, memories, ambitions. This one was perhaps reflecting on the principles and meaning that inform the struggle; this one, more aware of a physical discomfort, considers, maybe, a family problem. This other, again, weighs up his team's chances in the match that coming Saturday. What switch is pulled to join these brains into the circuits of a common purpose?

Now the Co-ordinating Committee has taken its place. Jim Cloughley of the Publicity Committee makes some final adjustments to the tape recorder which is to preserve the meeting, and Jim Airlie prepares to start proceedings. Powerful of physique and voice, Jim Airlie was a military policeman during his period of national service. 'That was before I learned how to think,' he responds, whenever he is chaffed about this fact. Now a steward in the Govan Division and Chairman of the Co-ordinating Committee, he is flanked by people of a remarkable stamp, the unchallenged leaders of men not easily led. Shipyard workers are renowned in Glasgow and elsewhere for their toughness and independence. The stewards have no formal apparatus of authority; acceptance of their guidance is entirely voluntary; their only weapons are words—and the proof they have given of their utter commitment to the men they lead. The words they speak from this platform pick up the situation that confronts them, shake it out and take it apart. They explain each concrete issue, its relationship to the Government, the Liquidator, the unions, the public and the men themselves. Their words mesh with the understanding and experience of the men they are addressing. They outline the areas in which decisions have to be taken, choices made. Thus it is not mere words that the stewards' leaders use, but words with understanding behind them, for the most skilful orator whose speech is not illuminated by thought is nothing but a windbag. In these mass meetings however, it is speech to some purpose.

The date is September 24. The Government has just announced that the Govan Division has been provided with a Board of Directors, preparatory to commencing operations as a separate business in accordance with the recommendations of the "Four Wise Men." The labour force is expected to accept this, abandon all thought of saving the two other yards, and enter into "meaningful discussions" on redundancies and working practices.

Jimmy Reid delivers the agreed report of the Co-ordinating Committee and the full shop stewards' meeting which always precedes the mass meeting. The demand remains the same: *all four yards and the entire labour force.* There are to be no discussions on future working methods, and absolutely no recognition of the Government's proposed board until these points are conceded. Certainly the dialogue will be continued, the Committee is willing to speak to anybody at any time, but it is not prepared, on behalf of the workers, to grovel and capitulate. UCS will stand firm, and the solidarity fight must be stepped up to ensure success in this endeavour.

The time arrives for questions and contribution to the discussion from the meeting. Once again the question of a sit-in strike is raised. The speaker is heard politely, but without support. Once again Jim Airlie explains the reasoning behind the tactic adopted; it meets with obvious approval.

But now an intervention of a different sort is being made. Someone appears to be in favour of abandoning the struggle and accepting the Government terms. Do they want the 2,500 in Govan to become redundant along with the rest?, he demands to know. Another cries out his astonishment at hearing such sentiments being expressed by a boilermaker. Is he not aware that the boilermakers had just taken a decision to refuse all redundancy? But the quitter persists, although by now hostility is mounting fast. The meeting is inclined to silence him, but the stewards insist that he be given the right to make his point at the microphone. He does so. What happens, he asks, when the struggle ends in defeat, as it inevitably must; why should Scotstoun and Clydebank drag down the Govan men with them, who now have a chance to survive?

Jimmy Reid's answer is met with roars of enthusiasm. 'I don't anticipate defeat, I anticipate victory.' He reiterates how the unity of purpose that has been developed is a stronger force than any Tory government. Nevertheless, they will co-operate with any meaningful proposals which meet the objectives of the campaign, not by accepting a worsening in their conditions but by releasing the ability—and in some cases it could be the genius—of the entire labour force.

Jimmy Reid was on this occasion too modest. These abilities and genius were already being released and displayed in the conduct of the work-in. On the basis of enthusiasm, understanding and organisation, a superb level of collective discipline was maintained. It was noticed that output and productivity were improving, though special efforts were not being made at that point to attain this. Pilfering all but ceased. Even the exodus from the yards at lunchtime and at the end of the day was more orderly than before. At the same time, the UCS men were keenly aware that the success of the campaign depended not solely on their own efforts, but on the maintenance of the support and solidarity of the movement outside the yards.

7
SUPPORT

The primary purpose of the five sub-committees attached to the Co-ordinating Committee has been to develop and extend, through their various functions, the support of the public outside the gates, in the first place that of the labour movement.

One of these sub-committees we have already met, the Finance Committee led by Roddy McKenzie. The fund-raising which they organised throughout the length and breadth of the British Isles and well beyond them represented the lifeblood of the struggle. Roddy told us that the number of donations received on an average day varied between one and two hundred, every one carefully recorded and receipted. There is probably no section of the labour movement which did not contribute.

> Brothers,
>
> Please find enclosed two cheques value £83.41. This being the latest contribution from above Committee and of course the members of our organisation. It is with great pleasure that I now report that the shop stewards last monthly meeting voted unanimously that our contributions should in future take the form of a weekly subscription from members. . . .
>
> You may remember that I visited the Yard during the beginning of the month. . . . At that time it appeared that UCS was in no danger of falling under the curse of mis-management whilst the workers remained in control. It must by now be obvious to all that the Co-ordinating Committee are doing a most professional and responsible job and may we take this opportunity of adding our sincere congratulations and entreat you to maintain the struggle for the RIGHT TO WORK.
>
> yours fraternally,
>
> **P. J. Lisle,**
> Convenor
> A.E.F. Shop Stewards Committee, Molins Machine Co. London.

Dear Mr. McKenzie,

I am writing to tell you that the following resolution was passed at this week's meeting of the Labour Party Staff Council:

"This Staff Council recommends to all members of Staff that a levy of 1 per cent be taken from each member's gross salary or wages, monthly or weekly as the case may be, and that the proceeds be sent to the Upper Clyde Shipbuilder's Fund . . . and calls for a similar gesture to be made by Heads of Departments and individual members of the National Executive Committee".

Forms have already been circulated for members to enter the scheme and I hope that funds will shortly be sent to you on a more regular basis than our occasional collections.

My personal best wishes in your struggle.

Ian Piper

Secretary to the Staff Council
The Labour Party
Transport House.

These two letters illustrate something of the feeling with which the labour movement eagerly levied itself to support the work-in. Any catalogue of its major organisations would at the same time list automatically sources of financial support. Of less well-known bodies, some examples chosen at random, include Cambridge and District Trades Council, B.O.A.C. Joint Shop Stewards, The Musicians' Union, Old Age Pensioners' Associations, Bank of England Printing Works, International Telephone Communications, London.

The Finance Committee made particular mention of what had been done by the late Bill Tweedie, Vice-chairman of the S.T.U.C., tragically killed in a car crash in December, in ensuring that labour organisations in Dundee were among the most consistent contributors.

Various trade union organisations abroad sent large donations, including the Irish Transport and General Workers' Union, and Soviet shipyard workers, who contributed over £15,000 up to the end of 1971. Owing to exchange restrictions, the East German trade unionists were unable to send money, but offered a free holiday to one hundred shipyard workers for three weeks.

The response of the general public has been, in Roddy's words, extremely impressive and moving. A woman doctor undertook to send £10 per week until the struggle was won. Hundreds of old age pensioners and unemployed have donated, among them a crippled ex-stage-artiste in Brighton whom the UCS delegation made a point of visiting when lobbying the Tory conference in that town.

Dear Jimmy,

The Old Age Pensioners of above branch wish to donate TEN POUNDS to the splendid fight of the UCS workers.

You are opening a new chapter in our age old fight against reactionary governments.

We appreciate the wonderful assistance given us in our own fight for a decent pension. . . .

With very best wishes for success in your fight.
Dan Docherty
Secretary
Cathkin Branch
Scottish Old Age Pensioners Association.

Schoolchildren in Aberdeen and Clydebank organised jumble sales on behalf of UCS.

31 Caiesdykes Crescent
Aberdeen

Dear Shop Stewards,

Please find enclosed £2 p.o. my school pals and I raised at a street Jumble Sale in aid of the UCS Workers. This was a hurried Jumble Sale because we felt you would need the money to fight that bad man Mr. Heath who is taking away your jobs.

We wish you well from Aberdeen.
John McConnachie (13)
Ronald Belsham (14)
Elaine McConnachie (10)

A much-favoured form of fund-raising consisted of concerts and shows put on especially for that purpose. In this the Finance Committee worked in conjunction with the Entertainments Committee under Ronnie Ferns, a welders' shop steward. The ex-boxing champion and boxing promoter

Peter Keenan laid on an evening's entertainment with premier wrestling celebrities and dinner at the Clydebank canteen, and this was oversubscribed at £2 a head; but perhaps the highlight of these affairs was the show put on in the King's Theatre, Glasgow on the evening of September 14. The stars of the occasion included Roddy MacMillan the actor, three leading Scottish operatic singers, folk singers Jim Craig and the Islanders, while Iain Sutherland, conductor of the B.B.C. radio orchestra, was the show's musical director. Special prominence, however, was given to four former shipyard workers who also took part, Johnny Beattie, the comedian, Glen Daly the cabaret artist, Russell Hunter, who appeared in "Callan", and Archie Duncan, an actor.

The organisers of the show were Equity, the actors' union, and its Scottish secretary Alex Clark—not an actor—handed over the proceeds to Jim Airlie at the mass meeting on September 24. These amounted to £500, the gross proceeds, for all expenses had been met out of advertising etc.

The Co-ordinating Committee not only received donations, but made them as well from time to time. It should be understood that these donations, such as that to the miners on strike, consist of money collected in the yards themselves, they came from the worker's own pay, and money donated to the UCS fighting fund was not used for these purposes.

There were, of course, forms of support other than financial. The Scottish Trades Union Congress, at the same emergency Congress that had resolved on full backing into the social consequences of the UCS closure, chaired by Professor Raymond Ilsley and including Frank Cousins among its members. Speaking before this enquiry, Jimmy Reid, while drawing attention to the fact that the terms of reference were unduly restricted—since the *consequences* could not be understood without examining the causes—nevertheless went on to present a very effective case on behalf of the men and the yards, pointing out that delivery dates were the best in Europe, and that Ridley had sought to intervene in the situation to suit the predetermined policy and programme he had hatched with his friends, Yarrow and others.

Indeed, all who gave evidence—workers, employers, academics—universally condemned the Government action. Scottish academics as a body are, lamentably, not renowned for their advanced political views. The Association of University Teachers' branch at one of Glasgow's two universities even voted to support Robert Carr's Industrial Relations Act. Nevertheless, by and large, even those who didn't comprehend the full meaning of the attempted closure were instinctively opposed to it, and many of them as individuals, and some in an organised fashion, made contributions to the fighting fund. One of the authors of this book attended a conference of Scottish university economists in September 1971 on the problems of the Scottish economy and observed that almost every person objected to the closure, though few had any idea of how to go about fighting it or what lay behind it.

One who was well informed was Professor Ken Alexander of the Economics department in Strathclyde University. He had formerly been a director of Fairfields during the "Fairfield experiment", and latterly of UCS itself. He explained to the enquiry that the case for contracting UCS was based on short term considerations, the consortium could certainly be viable if it were only given a chance and the necessary capital injected, for in the skills of its labour force it had an asset with which few other establishments could compare.

The maintenance of public support over a period of many months depended very heavily on the ability of the Committee to keep the public informed about what was going on. The greater part of the press gave attention only when "newsworthy" events were occurring, and frequently printed misleading reports. Two of the sub-committees in particular were entrusted with the responsibility for ensuring that the broadcasting of information was effectively carried through.

During most of 1971 the Publicity Committee was under the direction of Jim Cloughly, a burly, bearded engineer with a talent for Glasgow repartee, who displayed a particular flair for this type of work. This committee worked out ideas for posters, drafted and published leaflets and broadsheets and ensured that stewards who addressed public meetings were provided with adequate speaker's notes and all necessary publicity material. But the centerpiece of its work was the production of a weekly bulletin, entitled, modestly enough, *UCS Shop Stewards Bulletin*, produced in an attractive and professional-looking format, carrying comment and analysis on the current stage reached in the struggle. Some actual quotations will convey its flavour better than any amount of description.

Issue No. 4

"The Co-ordinating Committee are convinced that all our just demands can be realised, but to do this will require the vigilance and unity of the combined labour force. We know we have this unity. Our solidarity is an inspiration to all working men in this country and you have made us the recipients of the greatest support ever given to any body of workers".

Issue No. 7

"We are saying that without guarantees for the Four Yards there will be no negotiations, but at the same time we will discuss the Yards with anyone at anytime, providing the results are those which have always been our aim. THE FOUR YARDS. ALL THE LABOUR FORCE INTACT!"

Issue No. 9

"It is certainly not our intention to hand over any Division to be turned into a Training Centre, Bonded Warehouse or Womens' Lingerie Factory. With the close-downs in and around Glasgow and Clydebank, any potential businessman who is 'not interested' in shipbuilding will be able to find premises without undue concern as Glasgow and Clydebank are dotted with these derelicts. . . ."

Every issue of the bulletin included a sample of the names of individuals and organisations who had contributed to the fighting fund, and later editions included a cartoon by a young worker-artist, a painter at Yarrows, Bobby Starret. One of these shows an official at an industrial retraining centre addressing a group of redundant shipyard workers in this fashion: "O.K. lads, with retraining you'll be unemployed in two skills".

In keeping their case before the public eye, the UCS workers had an invaluable ally in the daily newspaper which more than any other consistently and capably did everything in its power, combating the difficulties of limited circulation, to ensure the success of the work-in. The *Morning Star* showed itself to be, at this time even more than normally, "the newspaper for all workers". In this respect the *Star's* Scottish correspondent Arthur Milligan deserves special credit. His reports maintained an accurate and up-to-date picture of developments taking place, and the necessity of this can be appreciated in relation to the fact that false and misleading reports were often spread through the other sections of the press calculated to chip away at the morale of the men and those in solidarity with them. They were generally composed to the tune that the work-in was collapsing, or that the stewards were capitulating on their demands.

"1 A.M. UCS. IT'S A DEAL SAY UNION MEN" cries a headline in the *Daily Express* of October 13, suggesting that the Govan-Linthouse plan has been accepted. Under the heading "GOVERNMENT OUTWIT STEWARDS AT UCS YARDS" the *Times* of August 28 wrote that: ". . . the Government have now clearly out-manoeuvred the shop stewards. . . . The 'work-in' seems destined to fail in its two objectives . . . more than 6,000 of the 8,500 jobs in the yards have probably been saved . . . the shop steward leaders are not likely to be able to weld the men together sufficiently to reject such an offer. . . ." The same correspondent of the same newspaper wrote on October 12 that "UCS work-in begins to lose its momentum", forgetting apparently that it had been "outwitted" and "out-manoeuvred" two months earlier.

A particularly unsavoury part was played by the *Glasgow Herald*, one of the two northern newspapers with an all-Scotland coverage, and one which consistently opposed the work-in, and even accepted the Government's definition of the situation. Although in its first reaction it declared, (June 11) that "UCS . . . have a stronger case for reprieve than is generally realised," it soon repented and by the end of July was pontificating on the theme that "There is always a time when reality must be faced and the West of Scotland has suffered grievously from attempts to postpone, even to avoid, the evil day".

This Tory newspaper was, in other words, prepared to contradict itself blatantly when it became obvious that the closures were going to be resisted by the organised strength of the working class, and its attempts to win cheap popularity by shedding crocodile tears in June, when all seemed hopeless, threatened to commit it to opposing a Tory policy. Founded in 1784 and therefore claiming to be the oldest surviving daily in Britain, it was, during most of the 19th-century, Liberal in political inclination, until the Irish Home Rule crisis in the 1880's pushed it into the Tory camp. Originally the possession of the family firm of George Outram and Sons, it was, in 1964, taken over by Hugh Fraser the drapery magnate, since which time its tone has become, if anything, even more right wing. While it did not dare to come out with a full-scale witch hunt, it lost no opportunity to cavil and sneer. "Lemmings rush down to the sea in great numbers and drown. That is solidarity without reason and we could be witnessing a variant of it at UCS". (August 31). "Guarantees of creative productivity and 100 per cent co-operation yesterday emphasised their absence in the weeks and years gone by". (October 1)

Even some sections of the press which might have been expected to come out in full support were not exempt from a derogatory and cynical attitude. Founded in late 1971, the radical bi-weekly *Glasgow News* soon established a firm place for itself with serious analysis of local news and institutions and naturally devoted a considerable amount of its space to UCS. Its approach, though, left a great deal to be desired, for more than once it questioned the competence and sincerity of the stewards leading the work-in, suggesting that Reid and Airlie, like everyone else, "had their price", and in its issue of January 18-31 an article by Andrew Hargrave, Scottish correspondent of the *Financial Times*, argued that the stewards should enter into negotiations with Govan Shipbuilders without insisting on the maintenance of Clydebank as a pre-condition.

It was certainly fortunate that the men's supporters who did not have direct contact with the yards were able to learn, through the medium of organs such as the *Star* and the *Bulletin*, that there was no weakening of resolve, that was, remained and would continue to be, "all four yards, the entire labour force".

One element in the struggle on which great stress was always laid was the maintenance of personal contact between the UCS and as wide a body of their support as possible. It had the effect of keeping the reality of the struggle, lively and fresh, before the supporters' eyes, and trade union branches, students and others were equally anxious to meet in the flesh these renowned contenders for the right to work.

All requests for speakers to outside bodies were handled by the Administrative Committee, during 1971 under the chairmanship of James Kilpatrick, a D.A.T.A. man. In addition this committee made all internal organisational arrangements such as the preparation of mass meetings and passing on to the other sub-committees information about events involving any of their responsibilities. Hundreds of requests were submitted to it from all over Britain and from Holland and East Germany. The committee then took the decision as to who should be sent and from which yard. Once that was fixed and the necessary travel arrangements made, all necessary details concerning the speaker were supplied to the organisation he was to visit, his name, his trade and union, when expected to arrive, etc. etc.

Up to fifty such requests were dealt with every week, and the number has on occasions been as high as seventy. These "delegates" were normally sent out in teams of two, an experienced speaker and someone less so, in order to gain instruction in how to do it. James Kilpatrick told us that the development of hitherto inexperienced workers into skilful publicists had been astonishingly rapid, and Jim Airlie has noted that the UCS is developing "a team of mass orators".

A very significant pointer for the future development of the labour movement in Britain is the manner in which political differences have been transcended in order to ensure that the united front, essential to the success of the struggle, was not broken. How many industrial conflicts have been and are still being lost not for lack of basic strength but because disunity of purpose revealed itself at a crucial moment. That this was not allowed to happen at UCS, is perhaps, of all the great achievements of the stewards, their masterpiece.

In the first place it made certain that any elements in the official trade union leadership who were vacillating and might have been inclined to capitulate, were unable to discover any significant support on which to base proposals for a sell-out, and so were obliged to maintain publicly, whatever their private feelings, the stand for the four yards and no redundancies.

Labour and Communist Party militants, members of the Scottish National Party and those of no specific political attachment, worked together harmoniously to save the yards. Naturally, however, each Party continued to draw and propagate its own conclusions from the crisis, but this was not allowed to interfere with the primary immediate target. Numerous branches and other organisations of the Labour Party, besides donating generously, passed resolutions favourable to the work-in. Large numbers of individual members were prominent in the struggle, not only in the yards but in organising support locally and nationally. The stewards mention with appreciation the fact that Wedgwood Benn gave immediate backing to the work-in even before the Labour Party leadership had officially defined its attitude, and have also paid a particular tribute to Frank McIlhone, the Labour M.P. for the Gorbals constituency, who worked together with them in a self-sacrificing manner, seeking no publicity but continually putting the case for them in Parliament and in the local labour movement. John Gollan, General Secretary of the Communist Party visited the Clydebank yard together with Alex Murray, Scottish Secretary, and pledged the full support of the entire Communist Party in Britain for the UCS workers, saying it "would use all its influence and energy in support of your fight and your demands". The fact that Harold Wilson also declared in favour was noted with satisfaction by the stewards, although this was not allowed to obscure criticism where it was justified. Roddy McKenzie, chairman of the Finance Committee and a lifelong Labour Party member, bluntly told Wilson, when the Leader of the Opposition made his visit to Clydebank, that his policies and performance as Prime Minister had been one of the main factors giving rise to the tragedy.

The Scottish National Party also declared its support for the work-in, and its organisations were well to the fore among the lists of contributors to the fighting fund, although it tended to see the issue in terms of the persecution of Scotland by Englishmen, by a "Westminster Government" rather than as an attack on the entire working people of Great Britain by a Government representing capital, and only to be defeated through a united demonstration of strength reaching far across the borders of Scotland.

Ever since the Communist Party was founded in 1920, Clydeside has always been one of the major centres of its strength; many of its most outstanding leaders have come from this area, and it is of course no secret that many of the responsible officials in the Co-ordinating Committee and the various work-in committees are members of the Communist Party. In fulfilling their role in the UCS struggle the Communists have striven to deserve the same sort of confidence as has impelled the citizens of Clydebank to elect three of them, including Jimmy Reid, as councillors in that town.

From the beginning of the struggle the Party spread no efforts in mobilising its members to take up the question of UCS and its fighting fund in all organisations to which they belong, and has never ceased to expose the role of Toryism and capitalism in relation to the shipbuilding crisis and the general economic and political disasters of the present days. Within two months of the occupation a widely sold pamphlet, *UCS—The Fight For The Right To Work* by Alex Murray had been produced. In the Lanarkshire town of Hamilton the local Communist Party branch took the initiative in setting up a UCS Action Committee, which included representation from the Labour Party, the Labour Party Young Socialists, the Scottish National Party and the Independent Labour Party. The Action Committee conducted public meetings in the town centre, and went on to raise £400 for the fighting fund, a particularly successful example of the typical sort of action taken by the Communists throughout the length and breadth of Britain.

The election by an overwhelming majority of students at Glasgow University of Jimmy Reid as their Rector, their representative on the University Court, was another indication that the barriers artificially imposed through the distortions of the media between Communists and the people were beginning to break down.

In any account of the forces behind the work-in we cannot neglect consideration of the attitude shown by the wives and families of the men involved. Often enough it is through them that employers and the media try to strangle industrial action. In this instance they did not even think it worth trying on, such was the level of total agreement on the rightness of the action. Joan Reid, Jimmy's wife, summed it up at the beginning of the work-in in the following terms:

"If the men decide to occupy the yards then we women will be with them backing them to the hilt on Upper Clydeside. . . .

"I know quite a few wives with men at Brown's and usually when there's been a strike they've been more concerned about the home and the effects it will have on their families. But this situation is quite different.

"There's a lot of feeling about among the women folk. They feel as strongly about the close down of Upper Clyde Shipbuilders as the men because it affects the whole future of their entire families.

"They know as much, if not more, just what the closedown will mean to the community. The men hand over the wages, but the women have to make the money go round. They know what the final bill for this is likely to be".

It has been remarked that the proportion of women taking part in the two big demonstrations of June and August was far higher than is normal for marches in the city, and in fact the entire workforce of certain factories employing mainly female labour turned out, notably Glasgow's cigarette factories.

Churchmen in Glasgow, Clydebank, and throughout the West of Scotland were prominent both in organising and demonstrating support and in fund-raising, and on October 14 the Church and Nation Committee of the Church of Scotland declared that it was "greatly disturbed not only by the severe effect which the closure of much of UCS would have on communities already suffering from unemployment, but also by the Government's failure to appreciate the special difficulties and opportunities of Scotland", and continued, "It is difficult to avoid the conclusion that the Government . . . have acted so inconsistently, unwisely and without sufficient regard for the social and human consequences of their action that the effect is punitive".

Even some of the local right wing felt obliged to dissociate themselves, verbally at least, from the Government's policy. We have already commented on the case of the Tory Lord Provost, Donald Liddle. Another interesting example is the Scottish *Daily Express*. In its issue of July 30 it wrote under the headline "MONSTROUS" that;

"The Government's callously clinical handling of the Upper Clyde Shipbuilders' situation rightly arouses immense anger. Its proposed surgical operation must be vigorously resisted. Prime Minister Heath and Mr. John Davies . . . should understand that not every industrial problem can be solved by "lame duck" euthanasia.

"Shipbuilding is a special case. Foreign governments do not hesitate to support their shipyards. It is up to the British Government to match competitors".

True, this number of the paper still referred to the stewards as "wildcats", and predicted in capital letters that the proposed work-in would do nothing except, "win a few days' publicity that will avail them nothing and that will pay dividends only in the pages of *Pravda* and the councils of the Kremlin". The following day however, the *Express* reported the occupation in an entirely objective tone, "quiet but unique revolution", and printed withal a flattering pen-portrait of Jimmy Reid; "great intelligence and drive and massive ability and determination".

We should not, however, imagine the situation as one in which active men and stewards in the yards were passively supported by a general public, which was otherwise of little account except for fund-raising. On the contrary, the UCS supporters could on specific occasions express themselves in an extremely active way, as on the two demonstrations. Besides, the consciousness inside the yards as to how the masses looked upon them not merely served to stiffen the morale of the workers, but inspired in them also the determination not to let down the hundreds of thousands who had placed so great a confidence in them and to justify the reputation gained throughout the labour movement by their action. The stewards kept this point continually to the forefront, and any expression of sectarianism towards other workers, public figures, political organisations or religious bodies was met with the response 'How do you know they're not contributing to the fund?' It was the combined consciousness of their own strength and the assurance of the solidarity of the wider movement that enabled the many manoeuvres and strategems that the Government now resorted to, to be faced and defeated.

8

THE GOVERNMENT MANOEUVRES

Having failed initially to secure the acquiescence of the UCS workers in the dismemberment of the enterprise and their passive consent to the removal of their livelihood, the Tory Government resorted to a great many strategems in its diligent efforts to divide and demoralise its opponents on the Clyde.

The regularly pursued tactic was to try to rupture the unity prevailing in the yards by suggesting that certain jobs or certain units in the consortium could be saved at the expense of others; "half a loaf is better than no bread", as the *Glasgow Herald* put it; and after each move by the Government, inspired reports usually appeared in the press suggesting that solidarity was weakening. It was a long time before Davies and his colleagues renounced their particular determination to see the Clydebank yard destroyed whatever might happen to the others. Attempted cajolery was combined with intimidation and bluster; for example, Sir John Eden, Minister for Industry, threatened in August that "continued intransigence and refusal to face facts" would "put at risk the security of countless families", and the threat was held out time and again that unless the workforce gave in and complied with whatever the Government wished to do, Govan and Linthouse would be closed down as well, with *every* job abolished.

In the month of August the Scottish industrialist Archibald Kelly, or "Scrap-iron Kelly" as he was more popularly known, from his practice of taking over and rejuvenating bankrupt establishments, proposed to take over the four yards as a going concern, provided he could get the necessary Government financial assistance. Though suspecting that Mr. Kelly's interests were as much in the resultant publicity (which he certainly got) as in saving the yards, the stewards were willing to undertake negotiations, but the Government sabotaged whatever possibilities might have existed by refusing to contribute anything towards Kelly's plan. John Davies piously remarked that the proposals he had submitted were "not credible", and that he "had little idea of what he will build in them or for whom".

On September 22 the Government announced the proposed management of its Govan-Linthouse project, the two yards that were to be hived off and retained with a reduced labour force. The declaration that the Department of Trade and Industry intended thus to go ahead represented a direct defiance of and challenge to the demands of the UCS workers and the feelings of the public generally. As Chairman, Davies nominated Hugh Stenhouse, insurance broker and former Treasurer of the Tory Party in Scotland; as Managing Director, Archibald Gilchrist, a former engineering manager at Barclay Curle shipyard. Others included Robin MacLellan, President of the Glasgow Chamber of Commerce; Ronald Lyon, Chairman of a company running private industrial estates; and the Managing Director of the merchant bank Noble Grossart. Ken Douglas, the previous Managing Director of UCS, whose competence had won respect on all sides and who was mainly responsible, from the management end, for arresting the early decline in the consortium, was not nominated to this new Board at first, possibly because he had expressed himself too sympathetically to the workers, though he later joined as Vice-Chairman. Jimmy Reid, reporting to the next mass meeting, commented that the set-up was an obvious "jobs for the boys" creation, reminiscent of a Monty Python sketch, and that the combined knowledge of these individuals in a shipbuilding sense was such as to make the proposals a joke in bad taste. Bob Dickie, Convenor of stewards at Clydebank, remarked that 'we are back to the same type of Board which lost millions in UCS'.

Nonetheless, even this piece of low comedy might have been made into the basis for some concrete progress if the Government had accepted the point on redundancies and incorporated all of the four yards into the scheme. Initially, indeed, Stenhouse immediately after his appointment was to declare that no obstacles would be placed in his way if he wished to acquire Scotstoun and Clydebank. Whether this was ever seriously meant or not is impossible to say, probably not, for on October 5 Davies informed representatives of the stewards and the Confederation who met him in London that the Government was determined to press on with the Govan-Linthouse scheme, making crude threats of the withdrawal of existing orders being worked in the yard there unless this was accepted by the men. The stewards then reiterated the stand which they had been maintaining from the beginning—four yards and all the labour force, no negotiations or co-operation with the new Board otherwise.

This had first been made plain within a few hours of Stenhouse's appointment when he arrived at the Linthouse H.Q. together with Gilchrist in order to see the Liquidator. The bad faith which lay behind the whole scheme was brought out in Gilchrist's explanation of why they turned up in a modest vehicle—an 1100 saloon.

'I borrowed it from my secretary' he said, 'We didn't want to turn up in a posh car at a time like this'. Never mind the realities of the situation. The decencies must be preserved!

Then the two would-be-directors approach the gates, where a group of stewards, with Jim Airlie at their head, awaits them. Stenhouse has enough sense to grasp the realities of the situation. He does not try to command; instead he enquires politely 'Can we get in?' Jim Airlie responds briskly, 'We are in charge of the yards and we decide who gets in through the gates. We are not co-operating with any Government Boards.'

Stenhouse then tries to make himself inconspicuous in a managerial sense: 'I am not a member of any Government Board. I am here as a private individual. I am visiting the Liquidator'.

'Then you are welcome to come into the yard to see the Liquidator. But I would ask you to make alternative arrangements in the future if you want to see him again'.

At this point Gilchrist comes in, ingratiatingly: 'I have not been introduced', and having insisted on shaking hands with Jim Airlie: 'I served my time here'. But he is put firmly in his place. 'Unfortunately you will never be Managing Director here'.

At the mass meeting of October 8, when he reported back on the Government's intransigence, Jim Airlie developed the same point. In a speech of fifteen minutes' length, delivered without reference to any notes, without a single pause or hesitation, and which raised the wildest cheering ever heard at the mass meetings, he declared:

'We will not bow before intimidation and blackmail. . . . The Tories cannot allow ordinary people to express their hopes and aspirations.

'If UCS is defeated then men and women everywhere will be afraid to say 'we have rights.'

'We will not fail the labour movement. We will not fail the working class. Above all we not fail ourselves. . . . All four yards, the entire labour force, no redundancies!'

The death of Hugh Stenhouse in a motor accident late in November gave the Government an opportunity, had it been seeking one, to think again, to restructure its plans and modify the Govan Shipbuilders Ltd. concept so as to meet the workers' justified demands and aspirations. Not surprisingly though, Heath and Davies gave no indication of budging an inch, but proved, as yet, inflexible in their folly. They went ahead to appoint Lord Strathalmond, a person with absolutely no experience of shipbuilding whatever, as part-time Chairman of their pet scheme. Part-time in good earnest! It transpired that the noble lord hoped *eventually* to spend as much as *one day a week* in the shipyard's affairs. The Government could scarcely have chosen a more calculated insult to the men and their stewards, who showed, however, in spite of it, admirable restraint and received the new Chairman with courtesy when he visited the Govan yard.

Nevertheless, behind its front of iron inflexibility, there was one important indication that the Government might be looking for a way out. In October it was agreed that Government backing would be given to the incorporation of the Scotstoun yard into Govan Shipbuilders if a "feasibility study" showed it to be viable, and would "assist in finding a buyer" for Clydebank.

So, as 1971 drew to its close, the work-in could claim two major successes. The planned rundown had been stopped dead in its tracks, and an unprecedented public opposition had been aroused to the idea of liquidation. The work-in was still rock solid and the fighting fund as sound as ever, achievements possible only on the basis of the skilled leadership demonstrated by the stewards, combining tactical flexibility with resolute adherence to principle; the ability and clear-sightedness with which the workers concerned carried through the campaign; and the effective backing of the labour movement and public inspired by this challenge to the Tory blight.

9

"AND NOW FOR SOMETHING COMPLETELY DIFFERENT. . . ."

By the beginning of 1972 a position had been reached in which each side, having consolidated its position, continued to watch the other warily. The Government awaited the "feasibility study" on the Scotstoun yard but still denied any intention of allowing Clydebank to be included in the reconstructed Govan Shipbuilders, and continued to repudiate any responsibility for its long-term future. In the other camp, the work-in continued with undiminished strength, despite reports to the contrary in the *Glasgow Herald.*

On January 12 an article appeared in that newspaper written by Ian Imrie, its industrial correspondent, in which he claimed that 1,281 workers had been declared redundant since June, but that only 263 of them were engaged in the work-in action. Thus he arrived at the conclusion that over 1,000 men had gone, a proportion of four to one against those defying the Liquidator. The *Herald* went on to sneer editorially that this "shows what value they (the men) put upon the chances of the UCS shop stewards achieving their objectives".

The allegation was quickly rebutted by Jimmy Reid, who also pointed to the malice which had inspired it. The *Glasgow Herald* figure had been arrived at by counting as redundant those who had volunteered for redundancy but who could not, by that fact, be regarded as part of the work-in. In actual fact, 'There are still hundreds of persons in the work-in. We are refusing to disclose the actual numbers as we do with the extent of our fighting fund', but, 'some sections of the community hostile to the cause of the workers seek to pour cold water on the actions of the workers to save their jobs'.

Another source doing the same thing around the same time is worth mentioning, if only for amusement; the sinister "Aims of Industry". This outfit is a pressure group financed in the main by the leading monopolists and dedicated to pressing for the most reactionary industrial policies and hunting out "agitators."

In a broadsheet published in February 1972 entitled *Power on the Shopfloor: Co-operation, Control or Chaos*, Mr. Frank Broadway claimed that the work-in was "quite a substantial step along the road to anarchy." He continued, "The use of materials or services without authorisation is unlawful misappropriation . . . nobody doubtless wished to see the unfortunate UCS workers hauled before the Courts (not half!) but we should beware of allowing emotive considerations to lead us to condone breaking the law." And presumably all the public institutions in the West of Scotland, including the Clydebank police who assisted in routing traffic through to the mass meetings, are to be charged as accessories before or after the fact.

No doubt the Government would have been all too pleased to see the work-in begin to crumble; its own position was none too comfortable, with public sympathy swung almost entirely to the side of the workers, and other industrial trouble, especially in the shape of the miners, coming up fast over the horizon. In spite of its apparently intransigent stand during the previous summer, the ground had ever since been shifting under its feet to such an extent that the actual position as the new year opened bore little relation to that which had prevailed six months earlier.

The idea that seven-tenths of the workforce should be forced into redundancy regardless of all other considerations was being quietly abandoned, no more was heard of the "Four Wise Men" and their report, while the potential scope of the Govan Shipbuilders was being extended far beyond its original conception. In addition to the feasibility study under way at Scotstoun, Strathalmond, the new Chairman, had made it clear that something like £25-£30 million would be necessary to get Govan Shipbuilders off the ground, and the Government did not contradict him, though neither did it make any definite promises at this stage. In assessing the achievement of the work-in it is worth reflecting on the difference between the £6 million which the Government had refused out of hand in July and the £30 million or so which it now appeared to be prepared to consider for only part of the consortium. So far as Clydebank was concerned, it appeared that the answer to the problem might come from the direction of the USA. Once again it was the stewards and the unions who shouldered the main responsibilities for handling these developments, the Government played little more than a spectator role.

The US-Belgian firm of Breaksea Tankers had for some time been expressing interest in the yard, particularly for the construction of liquid gas carriers, and was subsequently joined by the Marathon Manufacturing Company, the world's biggest oil-rig building outfit, and some others.

The development of American interest in Clydebank was particularly notable, for it demonstrated beyond any doubt that, contrary to what the Government and its advisory committee had asserted so loudly in July, Clydebank was potentially viable in orthodox commercial terms, otherwise it is inconceivable that the thoroughly capitalistic Americans would have shown so much interest in it.

Nevertheless, the ghosts of the "Four Wise Men" still stalked the pages of the *Glasgow Herald.* At the beginning of February 1972 a book on the UCS struggle, *The Right to Work* was published, written by Alasdair Buchan, and with a foreword by Harold Wilson. The book, written from a viewpoint very much in sympathy with the workers' stand, was reviewed in the *Glasgow Herald* of February 19. The reviewer concedes that the social consequences of a closure would have been catastrophic, but goes on to assert that there was "no warrant for assuming . . . that UCS was a potentially viable enterprise cut off just at the point where it was about to move into profitability".

This reviewer thus accepts without qualification the pronouncements of the "Four Wise Men" that, as he puts it, "By every normal and commercial yardstick the original decision was the right one", and considers whether the Government will be "*so foolish* as to pump £25 million into the still-breathing body of UCS". A thoroughly impudent series of remarks in view of the statements quoted in our previous chapters by individuals who might be presumed to have some knowledge of the situation—Ken Douglas, and Anthony Hepper, Managing Director and Chairman of UCS, Professor Ken Alexander, university economist and former director, not to mention the Shipbuilding Industry Board itself, whose final report confirmed the approaching profitability of the consortium when it was chopped down: ". . . with the end of loss-making orders, more settled industrial relations and improved production, the company should make the long-awaited return to profitability." The writer of the review certainly never produced any new evidence to contradict their estimate.

In the first weeks of January Dan McGarvey and Jack Service, Chairman and General Secretary of the Confederation, flew to Houston, Texas, to undertake negotations. The Confederation pressed hard to have a representative of the Department of Trade and Industry—preferably John Davies himself—present at the negotations, but the proposal was turned down. Nevertheless the two union negotiators reached agreement with the Americans that representatives of the companies involved would inspect the Clydebank yard, and undertook that in return for a satisfactory wage structure, demarcation boundaries between the trades could be relaxed. All this was explained by McGarvey in Clydebank Town Hall, at a meeting with local Confederation officials and stewards, so precipitating the most portentous and agonising issue which had to be resolved since the beginning of the work-in.

There were at this time three ships lying in the yards, one at each, which were nearing completion. The farthest advanced was the *New Westminster City* at Govan, and it was ready for delivery. The Co-ordinating Committee had taken a decision in November that it would not permit any of them to be delivered unless and until serious discussions with guarantees had begun on the future of all four yards. The question was whether, in view of the new developments, that decision should now be reversed, and the *New Westminster City* permitted to go as a gesture of good faith.

In the Co-ordinating Committee meeting of January 24 there is full awareness of what is at stake. Opinions are divided, for while some are in favour of releasing the ship, others feel that the time for showdown with the Government has now arrived. Everyone who speaks is heard with attention and respect, for there is no question of a division on principle, it is a matter of which *tactics* are the most appropriate ones to bring forward at this point. The situation is more ambiguous, complex and delicate than at any previous stage. Every person in the leadership must exercise his own judgment here, and it is understandable that opinions differ. At last the time for voting arrives, and the verdict is in favour of releasing the ship, a decision subsequently confirmed by a full meeting of stewards.

The final decision, however, rests with the men themselves, having heard why the stewards arrived at their recommendation. Jimmy Reid speaks with power and conviction.

'. . . I'm all for standing on my own feet even if we get beat, but by Christ I'd rather still be standing on my feet and winning, and that's what we've got to try and do.

'Sammy Gilmore said that if we did anything to lose the U.S. bid for Clydebank and the jobs there the punters will strangle us, and he's right, and they'd be right as well.

'We've got to make sure that the Government get no pretext for saying that these obscurantist saboteurs the shop stewards and workers have blasted negotations.'

The vote to accept the stewards recommendations is overwhelming. The Liquidator for his part agrees that further redundancies will be discontinued meantime until negotations have proceeded further.

In the beginning of February the outlines of a solution began to take shape, following the pattern of a reconstituted Govan Shipbuilders Ltd. including the Scotstoun yard, with £30 million or so of Government money to get it started, while Clydebank would be purchased by a U.S. company, assuming that the Government agreed to assist with the financing of capital development.

On February 28, with the Government still reeling from the battering it had just taken from the miners, and with its popularity, according to the pollsters, at an all-time low, John Davies rose in the House of Commons in the course of an unemployment debate to sing in an entirely different tune from that which had so charmed the Tory benches back in the far-off days of June and July. He announced that Govan Shipbuilders Ltd would incorporate the three Glasgow yards and be provided from Government sources with £17 million to cover inherited losses and a further £18 million for capital development, a sum even exceeding that which had been anticipated. At the same time he promised unspecified financial assistance to any private buyer for Clydebank. Wayne Harbin of Marathon had already announced that he was only waiting for a satisfactory telephone call from John Eden to begin taking serious action.

Speaking on T.V. the same evening Jimmy Reid expressed satisfaction with the outcome. He told the interviewer that it appeared to him that what remained were essentially "questions of detail". Asked when the work-in would be terminated he indicated that this could be done as soon as the future was assured for Clydebank. It was the second major working-class victory in as many weeks.

10

THE MEANING OF UCS

It has become something of a cliché that after UCS industrial relations "will never be the same again". In spite of this, the sentiment is perfectly correct. The tactic pioneered by the UCS men has quickly become a model for others, and at Plessey, River Don Steelworks, Fisher-Bendix and other places it has, with appropriate modifications, been used to great effect. The *idea* of the work-in represented a new departure in industrial action, showing once again the inherent resourcefulness of the working class and its ability to invent and devise new forms of struggle. Its *successful implementation* is equally significant. A book published some years back asked in its title: *Can the Workers Run Industry?* The answer emerging from UCS is that they most certainly can.

From the beginning to the end of the conflict there was not a single person who was killed, injured, or even assaulted. No riot occurred, no arrests took place, all windows stayed intact. For its scale it must have been about the most peaceful industrial contest in history. Despite all that, UCS demonstrated with an exceptional forcefulness that in the endless contest between the working people on the one hand and capital and its governments on the other, what counts in the last analysis is not persuasion, or eloquence, or even skilled negotiations, but *power*. The Government may or may not have been swayed by the strength of the arguments presented after July on behalf of the shipyards; perhaps they had a belated change of heart; we can draw our own conclusions on the likelihood of that. But does anybody seriously believe that the ideas of the "Four Wise Men" would have been discarded by Davies and Heath without the presence of, and the mass support for, the men on the ground occupying the yards, impossible to shift by force without unforeseeable consequences, regardless of the opinions of the bold crusaders at "Aims of Industry" on the illegality of it all?

The Government did not hold its hand because of humanitarian impulse. It has none. It refrained from physically smashing the work-in because it did not dare to act otherwise, and retreated when it saw that it could not wear the men down either. The two prongs on which it was impaled were respectively the situation in the yards and the attitude of the public, mutually dependent on each other's strength, and linked above all by the fighting fund. It was a process of continuous education, for which the greater part of the credit must go to the spokesmen of the men, who explained, soberly and convincingly, on innumerable occasions, not only before audiences of fellow-workers, but on a nation-wide scale in the press and over radio and television, just what was being done and why.

As indicated, the lack of physical disruption was not a sign of weakness but the reverse, a pointer to the wholehearted commitment and lack of serious opposition in the locality. The solid core of this community-wide support was the unity of the working class. Left militants like Bob Dickie (Associated Society of Woodworkers), Bob Cook (Municipal and General Workers Union) and Sam Gilmour (Electrical Trades Union) have worked on the shop stewards committees alongside men like Jimmy Airlie, Jimmy Reid and Sam Barr, all active members of the Communist Party's Scottish Committee. And the mutual respect which exists is shown by the election of Jimmy Airlie as Chairman of the Co-ordinating Committee, Jimmy Reid as Chairman of Clydebank Shop Stewards and Sam Barr as Convenor at Connels. Without this unity, pushing aside the right-wing bans and proscriptions aimed to keep Left Labour and Communists apart, the movement at UCS could not have developed into the massive campaign it did, involving all sections of the population. This unity provided the base for the fortress which UCS became, operating through the well-built organisational structure which furnished the framework within which the work-in was conducted—the Co-ordinating Committee, the mass meetings, the sub-committees, the publicity and the campaigns. In it was distilled the organising experience and the administrative lessons learned through their trade union affairs by generations of shipyard workers. Decisive leadership on the one hand, mass democracy on the other, is perhaps the formula which sums it up best.

Not only was leadership decisive, it was flexible as well, and this was no less essential to its success. As Jim Airlie explained on more than one occasion when voices were raised demanding that the shipbuilders should provoke the final confrontation, it was not the job of UCS to overthrow the Government single-handed, though certainly that outcome would be very welcome if the British people had had enough of its nefarious behaviour. But what the Co-ordinating Committee were concerned with was achieving the objectives of the work-in and they were prepared to set aside any particular tactic or subordinate demand if doing so furthered the essential aim.

The new form of struggle evolved by the workers at UCS, the work-in, corresponded precisely to the needs of the struggle at UCS, and this is a tribute to the ingenuity of working-class leaders with their feet on the ground, rooted in the day-to-day life of the Labour Movement. The work-in enables work on contracts to proceed. The control of exit and entry enables the men to frustrate attempts to declare them redundant, prevents the dismantling of equipment and retains the enterprise as a going concern.

The work-in demonstrates the power of the workers in a dramatic form which thereby raises morale and confidence. Furthermore it is a form of struggle which provides the workers with a period of time in which to secure the necessary financial and other support from wider and wider sections of the working class. The financial support is of course crucial, because as the struggle proceeds the work force has to bear the cost of wages for an increasing number of their mates declared redundant. This also makes it a crucial issue to develop solidarity action aimed at removing the threat of redundancy altogether.

The work-in is not an attempt to establish "workers' control" on a permanent basis. Such a conception would lack all credibility. But at the same time, it has demonstrated in a dramatic way the sense of responsibility and latent managerial capacity of the working class. In so doing, it has driven home in practice the important political lesson that socialism, a society without bosses, is not only feasible but long overdue.

The work-in, as we have said, had limited directives—to stop redundancies and closures. For the labour movement public ownership would obviously have been the preferred solution, and the breakup of the consortium was to be regretted. The fact that U.S. capital was having to be imported to bail out Clydebank can not be entirely welcome to a Scotland whose economy is already over-dependent on American enterprise.

These questions were raised at some of the mass meetings, and Jimmy Reid, replying on October 15 to one such, explained,

'We're not being party to any sell-out of a struggle and a movement that has lifted the working class struggle of this country to a new level and a new dimension . . . (if we insisted on the maintenance of the four *as a unit*) we'd be crucified as wretched dogmatists, because we're arguing and we're fighting for the right to work and if we win that, that quibble that our economic analysis is marginally superior to some other arrangement that's been made;—I'm telling you boys, we'd be on our own, we'd be kicked from pillar to post.

'The important thing is to retain these four divisions and our jobs. . . . There's not a worker in Britain that can pick his employer . . . that's the reality of the situation'.

In a situation in which panic, despair, or overconfidence would have been all too easy, the leadership kept its cool, and the Government found no opportunity for the successful employment of force or guile to the defeat of the men and the destruction of their undertaking.

UCS will doubtlessly take its place, along with such events

as the Tolpuddle Martyrs or the great dockers' strike of 1889, among the classic episodes of labour history in Britain.

Speaking for the UCS stewards at the special Congress of the Scottish T.U.C. on August 16, 1971, Jimmy Reid summed up the wider implications of the UCS struggle:

'It is time,' he said, 'that the working class wrote a charter of rights, at the heart of which would be the right to work. If the Government cannot guarantee that right, and if the social system cannot guarantee that right, then we must change the Government or modify the system'.

Or again, when reporting to the Glasgow meeting of shop stewards from all over Britain on August 10, 1971:

'At last a section of workers has reasserted the dignity of man. The UCS workers have struck a responsive chord in the hearts and minds of workers not only in Britain but throughout the world. This fight has become the battleground between economic policies that belong to the *laissez-faire* of the 19th-century, and social and economic policies which say that people are much more important than profits'.

The right to work, and to earn enough for a decent life without excessive hours of work, is an elementary right to which every worker is entitled, especially in an age when technology has the potential of creating abundance for all. That was the message of UCS. Redundancy was no longer negotiable. Everyone had the right to work. With this revolutionary demand, the UCS workers transformed the fight against unemployment and raised the standard of a campaign to stop the Tory wreckers from destroying the jobs and livelihoods of workers and their families.

The people of this country have many hard battles ahead of them before the position is reached where it becomes impossible for hard-faced men in the seats of government or the monopoly boardrooms to threaten the livelihood and future of communities numbering millions. But if the lessons of UCS are learned and applied, the coming of that day can be very greatly hastened.